THE CLEVELAND WAY AND YORKSHIRE WOLDS WAY

with the Tabular Hills Walk

About the Author

Paddy Dillon is a prolific outdoor writer with 30 books to his name, as well as a dozen booklets and brochures. He writes for a number of outdoor magazines and other publications, as well as producing materials for tourism groups and other organisations. He lives on the fringe of the Lake District, and has walked, and written about walking, in every county in England, Scotland, Ireland and Wales. He generally leads at least one guided walking holiday overseas every year and has walked in many parts of Europe, as well as Nepal, Tibet and the Canadian Rockies.

While walking his routes, Paddy inputs his notes directly into a palm-top computer every few steps. His descriptions are therefore precise, having been written at the very point at which the reader uses them. He takes all his own photographs and often draws his own maps to illustrate his routes. He has appeared on television, and is a member of the Outdoor Writers' Guild.

Other Cicerone guides written by Paddy include:

THE CLEVELAND WAY AND YORKSHIRE WOLDS WAY

with the Tabular Hills Walk

by Paddy Dillon

2 POLICE SQUARE, MILNTHORPE, CUMBRIA LA7 7PY
www.cicerone.co.uk

© Paddy Dillon 2005
First published 2005
ISBN 1 85284 447 7

Photos by the author

A catalogue record for this book is available from the British Library

Advice to Readers

Readers are advised that while every effort is taken by the author to ensure the accuracy of this guidebook, changes can occur which may affect the contents. It is advisable to check locally on transport, accommodation, shops, etc, but even rights of way can be altered. Paths can be affected by forestry work, landslip or changes of ownership.

The author would welcome information on any updates and changes sent through the publishers.

Front cover: Walkers following the Cleveland Way along the cliff coastline

CONTENTS

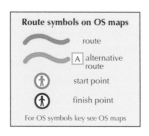

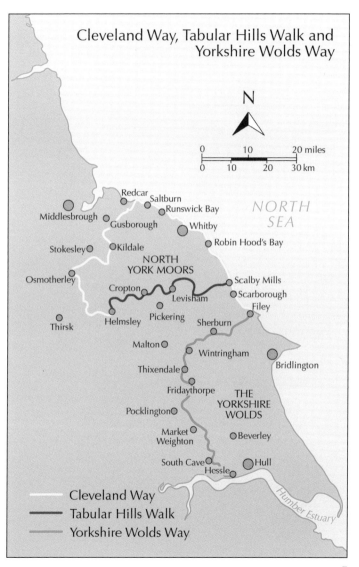

Cleveland Way, Tabular Hills Walk and Yorkshire Wolds Way

N

0   10   20 miles
0   10   20   30 km

Redcar
Saltburn
Runswick Bay
Middlesbrough
Gusborough
Whitby
NORTH SEA
Stokesley
Kildale
Robin Hood's Bay
NORTH YORK MOORS
Osmotherley
Cropton
Scalby Mills
Levisham
Scarborough
Helmsley
Pickering
Filey
Thirsk
Sherburn
Malton
Wintringham
Thixendale
Bridlington
Fridaythorpe
THE YORKSHIRE WOLDS
Pocklington
Market Weighton
Beverley
South Cave
Hull
Hessle
Humber Estuary

— Cleveland Way
— Tabular Hills Walk
— Yorkshire Wolds Way

7

The abrupt rocky western edge of the Cleveland Hills overlooks the lowland plains (Cleveland Way, Day 3)

INTRODUCTION

As a young teenager I pitched my tent for a week near Whitby, safely within sight of the chalet my parents had rented. One evening a man dropped his heavy pack to the ground beside my tent, and I watched in fascination as he sorted out his gear for the night. By the time I woke in the morning he was long gone. He was one of the first Cleveland Way walkers, and I don't know who he was or where he might be now, but I do remember wanting to follow him and see where that long trail went. My parents took me along the cliff path as far as Robin Hood's Bay, but the rest of the route remained a mystery to me for many years.

Eventually I got my chance to walk the Cleveland Way, and I have covered parts of the route many times since. I later walked the Wolds Way (recently renamed the Yorkshire Wolds Way), and the Tabular Hills Walk came last of all. I have now had the opportunity to walk all three routes afresh while researching this guidebook.

Each of the three routes is described in the guide, and walkers can complete them separately or link all three trails end-to-end in a long-distance walk of over 400km (250 miles). The whole distance could be completed comfortably within three weeks, even allowing for outward travel and return home. Together the three trails open up a wonderfully rich and varied landscape of cultivated countryside, intricate networks of dales, wild heather moorlands and dramatic cliff coastline, peppered with dozens of interesting little towns and villages.

The **Yorkshire Wolds Way** is usually walked from south to north, and extends over 130km (80 miles) from Hessle, near Hull on the Humber Estuary, to Filey. It traverses

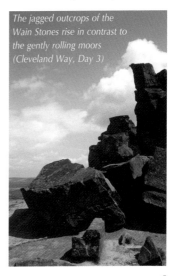

The jagged outcrops of the Wain Stones rise in contrast to the gently rolling moors (Cleveland Way, Day 3)

the Yorkshire Wolds, passing the villages of Welton, Brantingham, South Cave, North Newbald, Goodmanham, Londesborough and Nunburnholme. The central parts of the Wolds are sparsely settled, but the route includes Millington, Huggate, Fridaythorpe, Thixendale, Wharram-le-Street and Wintringham. The northern stretch of the route stays high on the Wolds, but passes Sherburn, Ganton and Muston on the way to Filey. For the sake of a day's march, walkers can continue along the coast to Scarborough and Scalby Mills to join the Tabular Hills Walk.

The **Tabular Hills Walk** takes in the gentle, forested or cultivated southern parts of the North York Moors National Park between Scalby Mills, near Scarborough, and Helmsley, far inland. The route measures 80km (50 miles) and wanders through sparsely settled countryside between Scalby and Levisham, then includes the villages of Newton-on-Rawcliffe, Cropton, Appleton-le-Moors, Hutton-le-Hole, Gillamoor, Fadmoor and Carlton. When the Link reaches the bustling market town of Helmsley, walkers can pick up the Cleveland Way and continue along this route back to Filey.

The **Cleveland Way** essentially wraps itself round the North York Moors National Park, covering 177km (110 miles). It traverses the high, western moors and hills at first, where villages are few and far between,

passing Rievaulx, Cold Kirby, Sutton Bank, Osmotherley, Carlton Bank, Clay Bank, Kildale, Slapewath and Skelton to reach the coast at Saltburn. From that point the route follows the coast and passes a variety of seaside towns and villages. These include Skinningrove, Staithes, Runswick Bay, Kettleness and Sandsend. The busy resort of Whitby is followed by Robin Hood's Bay, Ravenscar and the big, brash resort of Scarborough. All that remains is a day's walk from Scarborough to Filey to bring the Cleveland Way to a close.

Walkers who complete all three trails, whether one at a time or all in one long walk, will cover some of the most attractive, rich and varied countryside in this part of Yorkshire. The gentle landscapes of the Yorkshire Wolds contrast with the bleak and empty moorlands of the North York Moors, and the stark cliff coastline. Quaint little villages contrast with busy market towns and hectic coastal resorts; and always the next waymark and signpost beckon walkers onwards, trekking through Yorkshire's 'broad acres'.

BRIEF HISTORY

Around 10,000BC, during Mesolithic times, nomadic hunter-gatherers found a much different landscape than do today's visitors. The Yorkshire Wolds and North York Moors were largely wooded, with cliff coastlines facing the North Sea. Inland, vast marshlands were subject to seasonal flooding, so that between the mouth of the River Tees and the Humber Estuary east Yorkshire was almost an island, and certainly offered the only firm footing in this area. Flint tools are basically all that remind us of this period of occupation. In Neolithic times, about 3000BC, the land began to be cleared and cultivated, especially in the Yorkshire Wolds and Tabular Hills where the soil was more fertile. People were settled in communities and sufficiently organised to be able to construct burial mounds and earthworks. By 1900BC Bronze Age invaders had arrived in the area and their settlements were more defensive. These people continued to develop agriculture, but due to climatic changes were forced to abandon the higher parts of the North York Moors, which reverted to heath and tree scrub. Iron Age invaders came into the area around 300BC, followed by the mighty Romans from 71AD. With the Romans came roads, forts and efficient communications, and a string of signal stations was built all along the east coast. The Angles and Danes put the Romans under pressure from the 5th century, when the Roman Empire was beginning to fall apart.

Anglo-Saxon methods of cultivation were based around open field systems around villages. When the Normans pushed into the area in the 11th century the infamous 'harrying of the north' left many people as refugees on their own land, unable to call anywhere home or rear crops or livestock. Land was parcelled out among the conquerors and a series of fine abbeys and monasteries was founded, as well as stout stone castles. The Black Death of the 14th century left the landscape littered with abandoned villages, particularly in the Yorkshire Wolds. The wolds became a great sheep-rearing area and an immensely important producer of wool.

JET

Jet, often known as 'Whitby jet', has been used to create ornaments and jewellery since the Bronze Age. It is found in certain beds of rock that outcrop around the North York Moors, often along the coast, but also far inland around Carlton Bank. Basically jet is nothing more than a type of coal, but it is distinctive because it was formed from isolated logs of driftwood, rather than the thick masses of decayed vegetation that form regular coal seams. High-quality jet is tough and black, can be turned on a lathe or carved, and takes a high polish. Jet has been used to create everything from intricately carved statuettes to shiny beads and facetted stones for jewellery. Jet crafting has long centred on Whitby, with production peaking in the 19th century.

In the 16th century the North York Moors became a large-scale producer of alum (a valuable salt used as a fixative in the dyeing process) and vast areas of land became part of what was in effect a huge, early chemical industry that spanned two-and-a-half centuries. Alum quarrying was mainly located along the coast and the cliff edges of the Cleveland

ALUM

Throughout the North York Moors National Park walkers encounter huge piles of flaky pink shale dumped on the landscape, sometimes along the western fringes of the Cleveland Hills, but more especially along the coast. These are the remains of a large-scale chemical industry that thrived from 1600 to 1870. The hard-won prize was alum, a valuable salt that could be extracted from certain beds of shale by a tortuous and time-consuming process.

Wherever the shale occurred it was extensively quarried. Millions of tons were cut, changing the shape of the landscape considerably, especially along the coast. Wood, and in later years coal, was mixed in layers with the broken shale, and great piles like small hills were fired and kept burning for months – or even for a whole year. Burnt shale was put into huge tanks of water to soak – a process known as leaching – then the water was drawn off and boiled, which required more wood and coal, as well as treatment with such odious substances as human urine, brought to the area from as far away as London. As crystals of precious alum began to form, the process ended with a purification stage before the end product was packed for dispatch.

Alum had many uses, but was chiefly in demand as a fixative for dyes, allowing cloth to be strongly coloured and colour-fast after washing. The Italians had a virtual monopoly on the trade until the alum shale of Yorkshire was exploited from 1600. The local industry went into a sudden decline when other sources of alum and more advanced dyeing methods were discovered from 1850. The long and involved process of quarrying, burning, leaching, boiling, crystallisation and purification was replaced by other simpler, cheaper and faster means of production.

The main alum-producing sites along the course of the Cleveland Way are evident around Carlton Bank, Slapewath, Boulby Cliff, Kettleness, Sandsend, Saltwick Bay and Ravenscar. Others are close to hand and there are some two dozen sites scattered across the landscape. Look on these stark remains, consider the toil and labour, and bear in mind that it all took place so that fine gentlemen and ladies could wear brightly coloured clothes!

Hills, the interior being largely a wasteland crisscrossed by trading routes where no one was inclined to linger for long. To aid travellers across the moors, stone waymark crosses were planted. Settlement remained confined to the dales, with the moors bleak and barren. Just as alum production drew to a close, ironstone production reached its peak.

The 18th century saw the Yorkshire Wolds switch from sheep rearing to intensive agriculture, with the higher ground divided into huge, square fields planted with cereals. The Tabular Hills were cultivated in similar fashion, though the broader North York Moors began to be managed more for sport, with grouse shooting pre-eminent. Scrub was cleared and vast areas selectively burnt to encourage the growth of heather, providing suitable cover and

feeding for grouse, to the delight of 19th-century sportsmen. In the 20th century moorland began to be ploughed and planted, or 'improved' as pasture for grazing sheep and cattle, but following the establishment in 1952 of the North York Moors National Park the process was largely halted.

WOLDS, MOORS AND COAST

There are three essential elements to the landscapes traversed in this guidebook. The Yorkshire Wolds are chalk uplands of no great height, intensively cultivated, with the appearance of an enormous patchwork quilt, but dissected by attractive grassy and wooded valleys, and sprinkled with charming villages and farming hamlets. These uplands are explored by following the Yorkshire Wolds Way.

IRONSTONE

Cleveland ironstone was mined and quarried from around 500BC, as evidenced by an ancient bloomery site on Levisham Moor (a bloomery site was where malleable iron was produced directly from iron ore). However, large-scale working didn't commence until around 1850, when moorland and coastal locations such as Skinningrove and Rosedale were exploited. The tiny coastal village of Skinningrove became known as 'the valley of iron' as a major steelworks was developed there. Ironstone from Rosedale was transported over the moors on a railway to be loaded into the blast furnaces at Middlesbrough. Huge quantities of coal had to be shipped to the area, while industry and commerce was hungry for the iron that was produced. The last local ironstone mine, at North Skelton, closed in 1964. Steelworks at Middlesbrough are now much reduced, while Skinningrove only just manages to remain in production.

Typical Yorkshire Wolds scenery of a rolling
chalk landscape planted with cereals
(Yorkshire Wolds Way, Day 6)

The North York Moors National Park is broad and undulating, flushed purple each summer, but bleak and wild when swept by winter gales. Stout stone villages nestle deep in the dales. The moors are explored using the Tabular Hills Walk in the south, as well as the huge loop of the Cleveland Way. Space and solitude characterise these moors, and while many walkers believe it is a wilderness landscape, the expanse of heather is in fact entirely man-managed to provide a favourable habitat for grouse. Extensive areas have also been planted with forests, though 'improvement' of moorland to create more farmland was largely brought to a halt when the North York Moors National Park was established in 1952.

The crumbling cliff coast is the third element, rising high above the North Sea, but cut by river valleys where fishing ports have turned their attention to tourism. The coastline from Saltburn to Scalby has been designated 'heritage coast' on account of its rich historical interest. The coastal Cleveland Way passes the start of the Tabular Hills Walk and also joins directly with the Yorkshire Wolds Way. Despite being of relatively low stature, never rising above 454m (1490ft), the uplands traversed in this guidebook feature several ascents and descents, some of which can be quite steep. Overall there is great variety and interest for wayfarers who attempt any or all of these trails, but Yorkshire is a huge area and this guidebook only covers one corner of it.

Much of the cliff coastline is designated 'heritage coast' and abounds in interest (Cleveland Way, Day 6)

TRAVEL TO YORKSHIRE

Yorkshire enjoys excellent links with the rest of Britain and can be easily reached by train, coach or car. Overseas visitors can fly to Leeds–Bradford Airport and connect with frequent rail or bus services to the larger coastal resorts. There are trains from Manchester Airport to Scarborough and Hull, and Yorkshire Coastliner buses run from Leeds through York to Filey, Scarborough and Whitby. East Yorkshire Motor Services buses run from Leeds to Hull. Overseas visitors arriving by ferry at Hull can easily connect with frequent rail or bus services out of the city, and Hull Trains offers regular daily rail services between London and Hull. Coaches in the Eurolines network can be linked with National Express services to offer overseas visitors long-distance coach journeys to Hull, Filey, Scarborough or Whitby from almost anywhere in Europe.

The busy holiday resort of Scarborough provides ready access to all three of the trails covered in this book – it has good transport links and an abundance of accommodation. The Cleveland Way runs through Scarborough, the Tabular Hills Walk is just north of the town, while the Yorkshire Wolds Way is easily reached at neighbouring Filey. Regular daily buses connect Scarborough with Helmsley at the traditional start of the Cleveland Way, and buses and trains allow easy links from Scarborough to both ends of the Yorkshire Wolds Way

at Filey and Hull. Few of Britain's national trails are as well connected to the public transport network as these, so if you don't want to there is no need to drive a car into Yorkshire to reach any of them.

How walkers choose to structure their explorations of the area largely depends on which trails they will be following – any one, two or three of them. If your walk finishes at a different point from where it starts, return public transport can easily be arranged to Hull, Filey or Scarborough, all of which are linked in a single short journey with each other.

TRAVEL AROUND YORKSHIRE

Railways

The railway system in this part of Yorkshire is less comprehensive than it used to be, a significant stretch of coastal line having been lost. However, the resorts of Whitby, Scarborough and Filey are all accessible on the coast, along with Hull on the Humber Estuary. Once inland the only place where railway access is likely to be of interest is at the tiny village of Kildale on the Cleveland Way. However, the market town of Malton is also served by rail and has connections with both Moorsbus and Woldsbus services. Rail services throughout Britain can be checked at any staffed station, or by phoning 0845 7484950, or by checking the website **www.nationalrail.co.uk**.

Moorsbus

Moorsbus is a network of buses linking towns and villages around the North York Moors with some of the more remote parts of the national park. All services run during the peak summer season, with some weekends fairly well covered at other times. Moorsbus could prove useful along the Tabular Hills Walk, or on the early stages of the Cleveland Way, in places where accommodation is sparse and a lengthy detour off-route might have to be considered. With careful planning several days' walking can be covered from a single accommodation base. Moorsbus services are heavily subsidised, and an all-day ticket that can be used on any bus in the network is remarkably cheap (£3.00 at the time of writing). Make sure you pick up a current copy of the Moorsbus timetable, published free of charge each year and available through the national park or tourist information centres in the area.

Woldsbus

Like Moorsbus, the Woldsbus service attempts to open up the Yorkshire Wolds to walkers, with particular emphasis on visiting many of the little villages along the course of the Yorkshire Wolds Way. However, this service is quite limited, operating at most once each way, Sunday and Tuesday only, even in the peak summer season. Woldsbus runs from Hull to Malton and Thorton-le-Dale, where it connects with Moorsbus

services. The return journey to Hull basically provides for walkers who have simply enjoyed a day's walk and then want to head home afterwards. If services are likely to be of use, be sure to carry the current leaflet giving full Woldsbus details.

Other Buses

There are two main bus companies whose services will be noticed on different parts of the trails covered in this book. The northern parts of the North York Moors National Park are well served by regular Arriva buses. The countryside around Scarborough is covered by Scarborough & District buses, which are part of the East Yorkshire Motor Services company. Buses in the Yorkshire Wolds are sparse in places but walkers are likely to notice the East Yorkshire services. There are also a few small, local bus operators throughout this part of Yorkshire, and some of their services are mentioned at appropriate points. Tourist information centres usually carry stocks of bus timetables, but online timetables for both of the main bus companies can be checked at **www.arriva.co.uk** or **www.eyms.co.uk**.

Traveline and Taxis

Walkers who need specific information about public transport links, not only in Yorkshire but throughout the country, can call Traveline on 0870 6082608. Try to anticipate your transport needs, and phone in advance to check schedules rather than leaving everything to the last minute. Walkers who find themselves in need of a lift at any point, and don't object to paying the going rate for what might be a very long taxi ride, can call the National Taxi Hotline on 0800 654321. This free service links with the nearest taxi operator in the scheme, then you can check their rates before making a firm booking.

ACCOMMODATION

Finding somewhere to stay along the Tabular Hills Walk needs careful thought, as places along the way are unevenly spaced and some of the villages are altogether without accommodation. There are specific accommodation lists for the Cleveland Way and Yorkshire Wolds Way, listing plenty of hotels, guesthouses, bed-and-breakfasts, youth hostels, camping barns and campsites that might easily be overlooked, especially if they lie a little off-route (but bear in mind that accommodation inland tends to be rather limited in some places). These accommodation lists do not carry full details of the hundreds of addresses that are available in the popular resorts, however. For these kinds of places contact the tourist information centre in each resort and tell them where you want to be based and at what price, so that they can offer suggestions. If you pay over the phone using a credit card they will be happy to handle bookings for you.

The *Cleveland Way Accommodation and Information Guide* and the *Yorkshire Wolds Way Accommodation and Information Guide* can

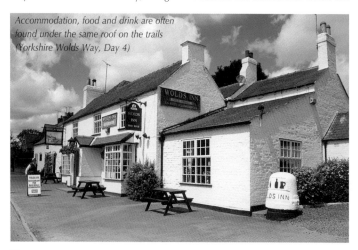

Accommodation, food and drink are often found under the same roof on the trails (Yorkshire Wolds Way, Day 4)

be obtained from the North York Moors National Park Authority, The Old Vicarage, Helmsley, York, YO62 5BP, tel 01439 770657. (These lists are sometimes free, but there might be a charge, so check first and send an SAE if required.) These accommodation lists can also be checked online and printed from the following websites: **www.nationaltrail.co.uk/clevelandway** and **www.nationaltrail.co.uk/yorkshirewoldsway**.

Please bear in mind that once you make a booking with an accommodation provider a contract exists between you. If you fail to show they may be entitled to keep any deposit you have paid, or even the whole sum if they are unable to let your room to anyone else. If you change your plans or know you are going to be late, phone and let them know as soon as possible. It could happen that your accommodation provider thinks you are lost and may worry sufficiently to alert the emergency services!

FOOD AND DRINK

The coastal resorts abound with a choice of food and drink that can be really quite bewildering at times, though the staple fish and chips rules supreme and the smell of deep-fat fryers can be overwhelming! Further inland, both on the North York Moors and Yorkshire Wolds, the choice may be much more limited, and indeed there may be times when nothing is

available all day long. Places where refreshments may be available are mentioned in each day's route description, though this is no guarantee that pubs, restaurants or cafés will be open when you reach them. It can be galling to walk for hours, working up a thirst, to find the village pub is closed, so always ensure that some food and drink is carried during the day. Some accommodation providers offer meals, but may require advance notice, and similarly they may offer packed lunches if notified at least the evening before. Places that do not offer food may be able to recommend somewhere nearby, and in remote locations may even be willing to drive walkers to and from pubs or restaurants, but it is wise to check if lifts are available when making bookings.

MONEY

While an increasing number of accommodation providers, shops, pubs and restaurants will take credit cards in payment, many don't, and walkers will need a certain amount of cash to cover goods and services while on the move, especially on the more remote parts of these trails. If unsure about carrying large amounts of cash, at least try and budget ahead, then be aware of any places along the way that have banks and ATMs. Many are mentioned in the route descriptions, and some supermarkets offer a cashback service.

TOURIST INFORMATION CENTRES

Many towns and some villages along these trails have tourist information centres and these are mentioned at the relevant points in the route descriptions – use them as the best source of local accommodation information. The larger offices may be willing to book lodgings on your behalf for a nominal fee, and they will also have details of local attractions and events, as well as timetables for local bus and rail services. Larger centres usually have detailed town plans, Ordnance Survey maps, guidebooks, and local crafts and souvenirs for sale. A selection of tourist information centres lying reasonably close to each of the trails can be found in Appendix 2.

INFORMATION WEBSITES

A good all-round website covering the North York Moors National Park is **www.visitthemoors.co.uk**. The Cleveland Way has an official website at **www.national-trail.co.uk/clevelandway** while the Yorkshire Wolds Way has an official website at **www.nationaltrail.co.uk/yorkshirewoldsway.** All contain plenty of information and feature dozens of links to further sources of information for wayfarers.

MAPS OF THE ROUTES

This guidebook contains extracts from Ordnance Survey Landranger

mapping at a scale of 1:50,000, with a clear route overlay. These are perfectly adequate for following any of the trails described. If you want to enjoy the wider picture and see where you are in relation to the surrounding countryside then you should carry some or all of the following maps: Ordnance Survey 1:50,000 Landranger sheets 93, 94, 99, 100, 101 and 106. For greater detail consider using Ordnance Survey 1:25,000 Explorer sheets OL26, OL27, 293, 294, 300 and 301. The appropriate Landranger and Explorer maps for each day along these trails are shown in the information box at the start of each day's route description.

WHEN TO WALK

Many walkers probably have an image of the North York Moors that includes purple heather under a blue sky. Such conditions may appear in summer, but bear in mind that the plateau-like nature of the area and its proximity to the sea ensure that misty days are common enough throughout the year. The Yorkshire Wolds, by contrast, feature ploughed fields, green crops and, in spring, brilliant yellow fields of oilseed rape. Spring is a wonderful time to walk these routes, when wild flowers are bursting forth and the weather improves day by day, but most walkers opt for the long, bright days of summer. The autumn months can be good, too, with russet hues stealing through the woods and

Seasonal variations in colour ensure that the landscape constantly changes (Yorkshire Wolds Way, Day 3)

across the bracken slopes. Winter is for the hardiest of walkers on the North York Moors, where snow can form drifts that hamper progress just as much as the short daylight hours. Even the gentler Yorkshire Wolds can be swept by piercingly cold winds, and paths along cliff tops may be dangerous when strong, blustery winds are blowing. A wet winter quickly turns some parts very muddy, though for most of the time the trails are along reasonably firm dry surfaces that can be used in comfort throughout the year. Badly eroded stretches, particularly along the Cleveland Way, were repaired and resurfaced many years ago and now provide a firm footing.

DAILY SCHEDULE

The daily schedule in this guidebook is merely a recommendation, and walkers are of course free to plan their journey along these trails in any way they see fit – it all depends on how far you feel comfortable walking in a day and what your accommodation options are at the end of the day. The route descriptions highlight intermediate towns and villages and mention if lodgings are available. Everyone has their limit, so if any day's walk seems too long, look to see if it can be conveniently split into two. Similarly, walkers with good stamina might combine two short days into one longer day's walk. Use the route summary in Appendix 1 to spot opportunities for combining stretches, or taking an early break at some point along the way.

RESCUE SERVICES

In the unlikely event that emergency assistance is needed, simply dial 999 (or 112, which is standard throughout Europe). State clearly whether you need the police, ambulance, fire service, mountain rescue or coast-guard, and be ready to give full details of the emergency. Ensure that you give your phone number so that the emergency services can keep in touch. Members of the public cannot request direct helicopter assistance – their call-out and use will be determined by the emergency services, based on the information you provide. As these trails often wander through remote countryside a small first-aid kit should be carried to deal with any minor cuts, grazes and other injuries along the way, and aim to be self-sufficient for the day by carrying food and drink in your pack.

TRAIL OFFICER

If any problems are noticed on any of the trails in this guidebook, please note full details and contact: National Trail Officer, North York Moors National Park Authority, The Old Vicarage, Bondgate, Helmsley, YO62 5BP, tel 01439 770657.

Erosion problems on popular parts of trails have been completely eradicated (Cleveland Way, Day 3)

THE YORKSHIRE WOLDS WAY NATIONAL TRAIL

The Yorkshire Wolds rise lush and green from the muddy brown shore of the Humber Estuary, and roll gently northwards before falling abruptly into the North Sea between Filey and Bridlington. The wolds are merely the northernmost extent of a broad band of chalk that stretches the length of England to Kent and Dorset. The chalk appears as sheer cliffs at Flamborough Head, but inland it forms a gently sloping tableland. This is covered by a huge patchwork quilt of intensively cultivated fields cut by a maze of steep-sided grassy dales, the latter used for grazing sheep and occasionally cattle or horses. The landscape is sparsely dotted with small villages and widely spaced farms – water was always in short supply, so no large towns could be supported.

The bedrock of the Yorkshire Wolds is porous chalk, laid down in the Cretaceous period some 70–100 million years ago. Although the land does not readily support flowing water, glacial melt-water flowed vigorously after the ice age and cut many valleys deep into the landscape. Flint occurs as nodules in beds of chalk and is easily spotted whenever the land is ploughed. The first settlers used flint for sharp-edged scrapers, blades and arrowheads. Several ancient settlement sites occur on the wolds, along with burial mounds and as yet unexplained earthworks. There are also deserted village sites, either abandoned during the Black Death of the 14th century or fallen idle due to changes in agricultural practices. The wolds are fertile, but as the soil is relatively dry and thin it is mostly planted with grain and oilseed rape rather than root crops, and colours change throughout the seasons. Towns are found on the lower ground, away from the wolds themselves, where water was more easily obtained.

Local members of the Ramblers' Association first suggested back in 1969 that a Wolds Way should be established, and in the same year East Riding County Council agreed that such a route should exist. The route had gained approval by 1971, but it wasn't until 1982 that it was finally declared open. Despite gaining national trail status the Wolds Way has always been one of the quietest of Britain's long-distance walking routes. The scenery is charming and interesting, but lacks the drama of high mountains, open moorlands, sheer cliffs and wilderness. In 2004 the route was renamed the Yorkshire Wolds Way with the intention of re-launching it in the public awareness. While it would be no bad thing for more walkers to experience and appreciate the route, as well as the wider Yorkshire Wolds, it has to be said that facilities such as accommodation, food and drink are sparse or absent over long stretches. However, such problems can be overcome with careful planning and the route can be enjoyed with relative ease.

Waymarks for the route are the standard national trail acorn logo, along with directional arrows. Signposts may simply read Wolds Way, or they may also include one of the next destinations along the trail. Keep up-to-date with developments and diversions by checking the website **www.nationaltrail. co.uk/yorkshirewoldsway**, and obtain a current copy of the *Yorkshire Wolds Way Accommodation and Information Guide* from tourist information centres.

Wharram Percy is the most famous of the deserted villages in the Yorkshire Wolds (Day 3)

DAY 1
Hessle to South Cave

Start	Hessle Station, grid ref 029256
Finish	Jubilee Clock, South Cave, grid ref 923313
Distance	21.5km (13.5 miles)
Maps	OS Landranger 106, OS Explorer 293
Terrain	Easy roads, tracks and paths along the coast, but note that one stretch is covered at high water, when a detour inland is necessary. The route runs through woods with some open fields later.
Refreshments	Pubs in Hessle and North Ferriby are off-route, but there is a pub near the Humber Bridge. Pub and restaurant at Welton. Pubs, restaurants, café and takeaway at South Cave.
Public Transport	East Yorkshire bus 66 runs regularly and daily between Hull and Hessle. Bus 155 runs regularly and daily from Hull to Hessle, North Ferriby, Welton and South Cave. Woldsbus services from Hull run through Hessle and Welton, serving many villages along the Wolds Way to Malton. Arriva trains run regularly and daily from Hull to Hessle and North Ferriby.

The Wolds Way starts on a low-key note in Hessle, almost as if it has lost its way before even going anywhere. However, things quickly become more scenic and interesting as the route progresses along the coast. Walkers are presented with a choice of routes at North Ferriby – depending on the state of the tide you can either make a beach walk or a road walk to continue. There are well-wooded areas on the way to and from the village of Welton, and open, cultivated countryside interspersed with more wooded areas occurs later. Slopes are fairly gentle for the most part. Villages are always just off-route during this day's walk, so anyone wishing to admire their cute cottages and fine old houses will need to make short detours. Brantingham offers food and drink, but South Cave has more choice and also provides accommodation.

Starting from the railway station at **Hessle** cross the foot-bridge over the busy A63 then turn left along **Livingstone Road**. The former **Ferryboat Inn**, now an Italian restaurant, stands on a corner where a right turn reveals the first Wolds Way marker post beside a telephone box. A short path leads quickly to the **Humber Estuary**

Map continues p.31

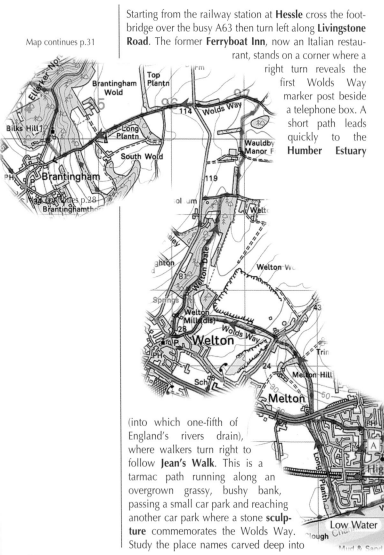

(into which one-fifth of England's rivers drain), where walkers turn right to follow **Jean's Walk**. This is a tarmac path running along an overgrown grassy, bushy bank, passing a small car park and reaching another car park where a stone **sculpture** commemorates the Wolds Way. Study the place names carved deep into

26

the stone, as these will become familiar during the week ahead and may even become favourite places to be recalled with affection. Follow the coastal road towards the graceful span of the **Humber Bridge**, marvelling at its size and architecture and passing one of its towering supports embedded deep in the ground.

THE HUMBER BRIDGE

A tunnel and railway bridge had been proposed long before the current road bridge over the Humber was approved. Opened in 1981, it was at the time the longest single-span bridge in the world. The length of road between the two supports is 2.2km (1.4 miles) and the cost of the bridge was £91 million. There is a special viewing area and visitor centre offering full details of the construction.

Pass the **Country Park Inn** on its seaward side and follow a clear track along a narrow strip of land hemmed in between the muddy shore and the railway. The **Riverside Walkway** becomes pleasant and grassy, passing a point where the remains of a Bronze Age boat were discovered. Near **North Ferriby** a decision needs to be made about which of two alternative routes to take, depending on the state of the tide.

Low Water Route

If the tide is out or the water is unlikely to cover the beach in the next half hour, then go down steps and walk along the beach. Avoid muddy patches and

27

slippery boulders, and bear in mind that the landward bank is private for the next 750m (800 yards) or so. When a wooded patch is reached climb up some steps, turn left and squeeze a short way between bushes, then turn right inland along a clearer path. This leads across a **railway bridge** and broadens as it continues through the **Long Plantation** to reach the busy A63.

High Water Route

If the tide is against you, then head inland past the **Reed Pond** and turn left along **Ings Lane**. Turn right along **Humber Road** and walk straight ahead to cross a foot-bridge over the railway line at **Ferriby railway station**. Continue straight onwards along Station Road and **Narrow Lane**, then turn left along High Street to pass a small newsagent. **Melton Road** continues onwards, then keep left to walk alongside the A63.

With the low and high water routes reunited, walk alongside the busy A63 to cross a footbridge near **Melton** then double back along the other side. *Don't try to cross the road directly as the traffic is far too dangerous.* Turn left up a path leading through **Terrace Plantation**, crossing a track to reach a private campsite. Follow a track away from the campsite, downhill through the woods, to reach another busy road at a gate. Cross with care and follow a broad and clear track straight uphill from a **quarry**.

Walk up the track until a Wolds Way signpost points left, then quickly turn right to continue alongside the edge of **Bow Plantation**. The path later drifts into the wood and reaches a junction of tracks. Turn left along a rather battered road called **Chapel Hill** which improves as it drops downhill. This leads to **Welton** where the Wolds Way turns right, but walkers may wish to go straight ahead into the village in search of food and drink.

Follow Dale Road out of **Welton**, passing a couple of **millponds** before reaching a lodge building. Walk through half-forested and half-grassy **Welton Dale**,

The graceful span of the Humber Bridge, looking from Lincolnshire to Yorkshire

WELTON

This fine little village has a vigorous, canal-like stream running through it, so St Helen's Church looks as though it is marooned on an island. The 17th-century Green Dragon Inn offers food, drink and accommodation, and this is where the notorious highwayman Dick Turpin was arrested in 1739. There is bed-and-breakfast elsewhere in Welton and the surrounding area, but the only other facility in the village is a post office shop. Woldsbus services link with Hessle and Hull as well as South Cave, North Newbald and Market Weighton. East Yorkshire bus 155 runs regularly to South Cave, Hessle and Hull.

St Helen's Church sits beside a canalised stream in the village of Welton

which becomes more wooded as you progress into it. Go straight through a clearing and follow the most obvious path to cross a concrete access road. Turn right to follow a path parallel to the road, then turn left as signposted Wolds Way to walk away from it. The path has a forest on the left and open fields on the right, and runs directly north to pass a pond so overgrown that it might not even be noticed. Turn left along a track and almost immediately right alongside **Wauldby Manor Farm**.

A clear track runs through fields and drops down to an intersection of tracks. Turn left as signposted Wolds Way and follow a path up through the shelter belt woodland of **Bottom Plantation**. Emerge at a road junction and simply walk straight ahead along **Elloughton Dale Road** until the road turns suddenly left. At this point walk straight ahead along a clear track blocked against traffic by tree trunks. The grassy track leads gently uphill beside **Long Plantation** as it rises over 140m (460ft) on **Brantingham Wold**. Pass another tree-trunk barrier and continue straight ahead along a minor road that soon begins to drop steeply towards **Brantingham**. The village is off-route but the road leads straight there if desired, otherwise turn right across a stile signposted Wolds Way to walk down a steep and grassy slope towards All Saints Church on **Dale Road** outside the village.

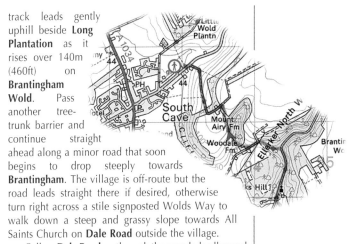

Follow **Dale Road** up through the wooded valley and turn left up a clear track. This climbs up through another wooded dale and reaches a gap between two small hills on **Ellerker North Wold**. Walk straight down a path flanked by wire fences towards **Woodale Farm**, but turn right to follow a track beside a tall wooden fence. Turn left off the track and cross a small wooded dale, then climb up a grassy slope. Continue uphill alongside the wood, taking care near its brambly edge. Cross a stile and watch out for a right turn, signposted Wolds Way, through the shelter belt woodland, followed by a left turn alongside it. Pass behind **Mount Airy Farm** at 130m (425ft) to reach a track.

BRANTINGHAM

Facilities in this fine old estate village are quite limited and you have to walk all the way from one side to the other to find them. There is a post office and shop, and the nearby Triton Inn serves food and drink. East Yorkshire bus 155 runs regularly and daily to South Cave, Welton, North Ferriby and Hull. Bus 143 occasionally links the village with South Cave and Beverley, but there are no Woldsbus services.

A grassy track runs by Long Plantation, over Brantingham Wold to Brantingham

Turn left along the track and walk down the farm access road, turning right to pass quickly through a belt of woodland. The road crosses a large field then turns left to drop steeply down to a lower road. Turn left again to walk towards **South Cave**. The village is actually off-route, and just as its outskirts are reached the Wolds Way is signposted off to the right, but most walkers will be happy to pay a visit and maybe stay overnight.

SOUTH CAVE

Dominated by its Jubilee Clock, South Cave is a busy little village offering a good range of facilities. The Fox and Coney offers food, drink and lodgings and the Bear is another pub serving food and drink. There is also a restaurant and café, and the village has a bank with an ATM, a post office and a few shops. East Yorkshire bus 155 regularly links with Brantingham, Welton, North Ferriby, Hessle and Hull. Woldsbus services link with Hessle and Hull as well as North Newbald, Market Weighton and onwards to Malton.

DAY 2
South Cave to Goodmanham or
Market Weighton

Start	Jubilee Clock, South Cave, grid ref 923313
Finish	Goodmanham Parish Church, grid ref 890432, *or* the Londesborough Arms, Market Weighton, grid ref 877417
Distance	19km (12 miles)
Maps	OS Landranger 106, OS Explorer 293
Terrain	Easy roads, tracks and paths with a few ascents and descents on reasonably gentle slopes. Route-finding is intricate at first but easier later.
Refreshments	Pubs off-route in North Newbald. Pubs, restaurants, cafés and takeaways at Market Weighton.
Public Transport	Woldsbus services link South Cave with Hessle and Hull as well as with Arras and Market Weighton. East Yorkshire bus X46 links Arras and Market Weighton with Hull and Beverley, Pocklington and York.

The Yorkshire Wolds increase in height as this day's walk unfolds, although the higher parts are simply rolling fields rather than hills. A series of charming, steep-sided dales are visited – some wooded, some grassy – two of which have had railways routed through them in the past. After leaving South Cave facilities actually on the way are very limited indeed, with the village of North Newbald located 1.5km (1 mile) off-route if food and drink are needed in the middle of the day. After passing the remote farmstead of Arras, which offers bed-and-breakfast, walkers are faced with a choice of routes. Either follow the main route to Goodmanham, which has a pub but no accommodation, or take an alternative loop through Market Weighton where there is a hotel and several opportunities to enjoy food and drink.

Leave **South Cave** by following **Beverley Road** out of the village, then turn left on the outskirts as signposted

33

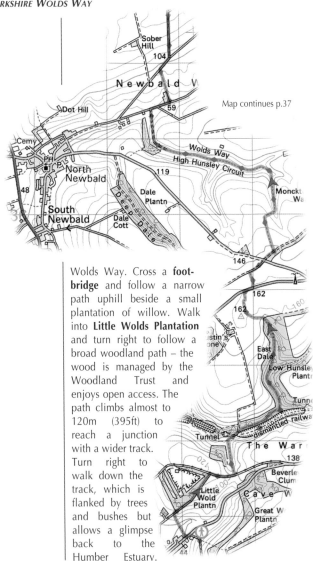

Map continues p.37

Wolds Way. Cross a **foot-bridge** and follow a narrow path uphill beside a small plantation of willow. Walk into **Little Wolds Plantation** and turn right to follow a broad woodland path – the wood is managed by the Woodland Trust and enjoys open access. The path climbs almost to 120m (395ft) to reach a junction with a wider track. Turn right to walk down the track, which is flanked by trees and bushes but allows a glimpse back to the Humber Estuary.

North Plantation, seen from the Wolds Way after passing High Hunsley Beacon

Watch out for a stile on the left where the Wolds Way runs down a grassy path through little **Comber Dale**. Swing right near the bottom of the slope to reach a bridle kissing gate – a huge kissing gate for horses (cross a stile alongside if unsure how to operate it).

Cross over an old railway trackbed in **Weedley Dale** (the railway ran from 1885 to 1959). Don't follow the trackbed but turn right as marked to follow a grassy woodland track above the cutting. The markers later point right, then almost immediately left, taking the Wolds Way up a woodland track through **East Dale**. The clear track later swings left and narrows as it climbs, while the woodlands become quite dense. Emerge into a field at the top and turn left to wriggle round the edge to reach the busy B1230. Cross with care and turn right to follow it to **High Hunsley Beacon** at 162m (532ft). A sign swinging from a brazier reads: 'Erected by Rowley Parish Council Queen Elizabeth II Golden Jubilee 2002'. Hunsley Beacon is also the name of a nearby transmitter mast.

Turn left alongside a field and away from the busy road, then right along a quieter road and head straight through a crossroads. Continue walking alongside a strip

of woodland known as **North Plantation**. Turn left alongside another field and turn right around its
boundary. Cross a stile and drop down into a
dale, then turn left through an **old
gateway** – no more than a couple of
stout posts in a gap in an old hedge.
Walk down through the dale
passing large clumps of nettles,
though these do not impinge on
the grassy path. The steep slopes
are used for sheep grazing. Turn
left at a Wolds Way signpost to
reach a confluence of dales and
continue down through **Swin Dale**.

Follow the path as marked, then
turn right as signposted Wolds Way to
follow a clear grassy track further down through
the dale. The floor of the dale is cultivated, while its steep
slopes remain untilled and trees fringe its upper brow.
When a minor road is reached the Wolds Way turns
right, but walkers who need food and drink can turn left
and walk off-route to **North Newbald**.

Follow the road from **Swin Dale** to a farm and turn
left up a clear track to a higher road on **Newbald Wold**.
Turn right along this road then left up another broad,
clear track. When the track levels out it passes a trig point
at 144m (472ft) and there are good views around the
higher wolds. The track narrows as it passes under a
pylon line and there is a Wolds Way signpost at **Gare**

NORTH NEWBALD

The village offers a few facilities in an area otherwise lacking services.
Clustered around the Green are two pubs, the Gnu and the Tiger Inn, both
serving food and drink and the former also providing accommodation.
The Post Office and Stores also faces the Green. Woldsbus services link
the village with Market Weighton and South Cave, or more distantly with
Hull and Malton. Use the road signposted Beverley to get back onto the
Wolds Way.

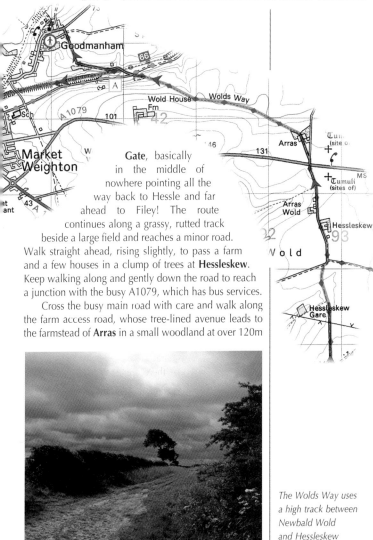

Gate, basically in the middle of nowhere pointing all the way back to Hessle and far ahead to Filey! The route continues along a grassy, rutted track beside a large field and reaches a minor road. Walk straight ahead, rising slightly, to pass a farm and a few houses in a clump of trees at **Hessleskew**. Keep walking along and gently down the road to reach a junction with the busy A1079, which has bus services.

Cross the busy main road with care and walk along the farm access road, whose tree-lined avenue leads to the farmstead of **Arras** in a small woodland at over 120m

The Wolds Way uses a high track between Newbald Wold and Hessleskew

(395ft). The farmhouse is on the left and offers bed-and-breakfast, otherwise simply walk straight through the farmyard to continue. The Wolds Way runs alongside enormous fields, initially tracing the overhead power line away from the farm across **Weighton Wold**. A grassy track later runs down a slope to reach a gate at a road junction. Walk straight ahead to follow the minor road to an intersection with an old railway trackbed, now signposted the Hudson Way, which is where a decision needs to be made about a choice of routes.

The main route goes to Goodmanham today and meets up with the alternative route at Londesborough Park on Day 3, but lacks all but the most basic facilities. The alternative route goes to Market Weighton today, which offers more in the way of accommodation, food and drink, and then rejoins the main route at Londesborough Park on Day 3.

Main Route

Simply stay on the road to follow the main course of the Wolds Way. The road climbs out of the wooded dale, swinging right to proceed at a gentler gradient. Turn left at a road junction to walk into **Goodmanham**.

Alternative Route

Turn left along the old railway trackbed, signposted the Hudson Way. The line operated from 1865 to 1965 and its founder, George Hudson, made and lost a fortune on the enterprise. Follow the track through a well-wooded

GOODMANHAM

This delightful little village surrounds an old church and features fine houses and cottages. Of particular note in the church is the lavish baptismal font carved with the words, 'wyth owt baptysm no soull ma be saved'. The only facility is the Goodmanham Arms, which operates its own micro-brewery from the back of the premises. Limited buses run to and from Market Weighton, but Goodmanham is one of the few Wolds Way villages not on the Woldsbus route.

dale. There is no doubting the way ahead, which is always clear and generally flanked by trees and bushes. The route soon brushes alongside **Market Weighton**. Watch out for a turning on the left that leads into town by way of **Station Road** and a passage beside All Saints Church known as **Church Side**. This leads to the main shopping street beside the Londesborough Arms.

The 'alternative route' follows the Hudson Way railway path into Market Weighton

MARKET WEIGHTON

This is the only town of any size actually on the Wolds Way, apart from Filey at the end, and it offers a good range of services. While considering its size, also consider the size of William Bradley, born at Bradley House on York Road in 1792 and buried in the churchyard of All Saints Church in 1820. He was the tallest man in the country, standing 2.36m (7ft 9ins). A life-size statue is planned to stand outside his birthplace.

The only place offering accommodation is the Londesborough Arms, but otherwise there are banks with ATMs, a post office, toilets, plenty of pubs, restaurants, cafés and takeaways, as well as a range of shops including one selling outdoor gear. Woldsbus services link with Londesborough, Arras and several Wolds Way villages between Hull and Malton. East Yorkshire bus X46 runs daily to Pocklington and York as well as Arras, Beverley and Hull.

DAY 3
Goodmanham or Market Weighton
to Millington

Start	Goodmanham Parish Church, grid ref 890432, *or* Londesborough Arms, Market Weighton, grid ref 877417
Finish	Ramblers Rest, Millington, grid ref 831518
Distance	14.5km (9 miles)
Maps	OS Landranger 106, OS Explorer 294
Terrain	Mostly low-level walking along quiet roads, tracks and field paths.
Refreshments	Café at Towthorpe Corner on the main route, pub at the end of the day in Millington. Pubs, restaurants, cafés and takeaways off-route in Pocklington.
Public Transport	East Yorkshire bus X46 regularly links Market Weighton with Pocklington and York, as well as with Arras, Beverley and Hull. Only a limited bus service runs between Market Weighton and Goodmanham. East Yorkshire bus 199 is a Tuesday-only run from Pocklington to Nunburnholme and Huggate. Woldsbus services link Millington, Nunburnholme and Londesborough with the towns of Pocklington and Market Weighton, as well as more distant Malton and Hull.

The Wolds Way was left split at the end of the previous day's route description, so walkers on the main route through Goodmanham and the alternative route through Market Weighton need to see both combine again in Londesborough Park. The day's walk to Millington is through undemanding countryside with no significant ascents or descents, and while facilities are scarce during the day there is the chance to detour off-route to the market town of Pocklington if a greater range of services is required in the evening. There might also be time to include a diversion to Kilnwick Percy Hall, now run as a Buddhist centre (visits available at certain times). Beyond Millington the Wolds Way features some strenuous ascents and descents, so walkers might appreciate this leisurely day.

Goodmanham's fine old stone church is on the 'main route' of the Wolds Way

Main Route

Leave **Goodmanham** by following the Wolds Way as signposted at the top end of the churchyard. The route leaves the village and runs straight down a track and under an old **railway bridge**. Continue onwards, swinging left gently uphill alongside a line of trees and bushes, then turn right to follow a clear track straight across fields. This reaches the busy A163 at the **Towthorpe Corner** picnic site. If refreshments are needed a left turn a short way downhill leads to the Woodsyde Café, otherwise simply cross the road.

The Wolds Way runs straight ahead through fields, continuing onwards using a farm access road. Watch for a stile on the left where a grassy slope leads gently down to another stile. Cross a footbridge between a small pond and the **Lake**, where waterfowl can be spotted – a rare opportunity in the largely waterless wolds. Walk uphill and follow a grassy track, turning left as marked along another track to go through a gate. The track continues through **Londesborough Park**, a pleasant, grassy area dotted with fine trees. The main route reaches a junction with the alternative route at a three-fingered Wolds Way signpost where a right turn leads up to **Londesborough**.

Alternative Route

Leave **Market Weighton** by following **York Road** – the main A1079 – out of town. Just as the outskirts are reached turn right as signposted straight across a field.

The Wolds Way continues alongside other fields, crossing small footbridges over a handful of field drains. These lower fields have deeper soil than the high wolds, and so can be used for root crops as well as grain and oilseed rape. A grassy track leads to the busy A163, which wayfarers simply cross to continue along a farm access road. This leads to **Towthorpe Grange**, which offers accommodation.

Walk onwards as marked and cross over **Towthorpe Beck**. The route runs through or alongside fields and generally parallel to the beck, though this is often unseen. A grassy track leads to a minor road where you turn left and then right to go through a monumental gate at a **gate lodge**. Follow a track straight ahead into **Londesborough Park**. The alternative route reaches a junction with the main route at a three-fingered Wolds Way signpost where you simply walk straight ahead up to **Londesborough**.

LONDESBOROUGH

There are no facilities for walkers in the village, though the cottages and houses are lovely to look at and All Saints Church is a feature of interest. The present Londesborough Hall is a brick-built structure, but in 1819 the Duke of Devonshire ordered the demolition of the original Londesborough Hall so that the stonework could be taken across country to build Chatsworth House. There are Woldsbus services to Market Weighton and Hull, as well as to Pocklington, Millington and onwards to Malton.

Follow the road through the village, passing All Saints Church. Turn right to take a road up from the village, straight through a crossroads, then across a gently sloping landscape of cultivated fields. Although the land barely reaches 90m (295ft) there is a **view indicator** to help unravel the distant features seen across the Vale of York. In clear weather this view stretches from Goole Docks to York Minster and Pocklington Church, taking in prominent power stations at Doncaster, Drax, Eggborough and

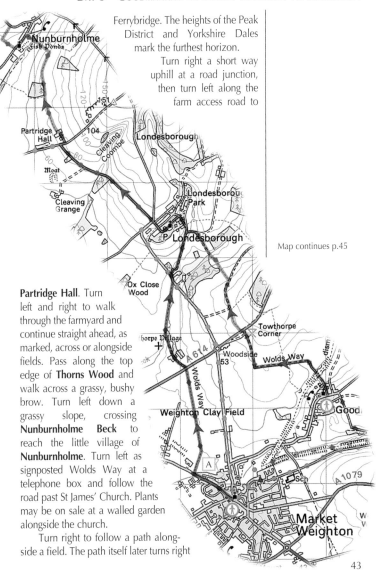

Ferrybridge. The heights of the Peak District and Yorkshire Dales mark the furthest horizon.

Turn right a short way uphill at a road junction, then turn left along the farm access road to

Map continues p.45

Partridge Hall. Turn left and right to walk through the farmyard and continue straight ahead, as marked, across or alongside fields. Pass along the top edge of **Thorns Wood** and walk across a grassy, bushy brow. Turn left down a grassy slope, crossing **Nunburnholme Beck** to reach the little village of **Nunburnholme**. Turn left as signposted Wolds Way at a telephone box and follow the road past St James' Church. Plants may be on sale at a walled garden alongside the church.

Turn right to follow a path alongside a field. The path itself later turns right

43

NUNBURNHOLME

Testifying to the antiquity of Nunburnholme, a lavishly carved Anglo-Saxon cross can be seen inside St James' Church, and it is worth obtaining the key to the church to see it. A 19th-century vicar, the Rev. Francis Orpen Morris, wrote the hugely successful six-volume *History of British Birds*. As its name suggests, Nunburnholme was indeed the site of a nunnery – the Benedictine Priory of St Mary. A 12th-century manorial complex has been identified, and there are Tudor earthworks and the remains of a fishpond. There are no facilities for walkers. East Yorkshire bus 199 is a Tuesday-only service to Pocklington and Huggate. Woldsbus services link with neighbouring Londesborough and Pocklington, and more distant Hull and Malton.

and reaches another minor road. Turn left to follow the road then right at a junction. A rather battered road climbs steeply uphill through **Bratt Wood**. Go through a gate and walk along the full length of a cows' field to leave at another gate on the far side. Continue through fields and follow the marked route through the farmyard at **Wold Farm**. Leave along the farm access road but turn right uphill beside a house. Turn left along the edge of a field to reach the B1246. A bed-and-breakfast lies off-route down the road, while East Yorkshire bus 744 runs to and from Pocklington and Great Driffield, otherwise cross over to continue walking as signposted for the Wolds Way.

Drop downhill a little after crossing the road and walk straight ahead alongside fields, though make a quick turn

A fine little pond in the heart of Londesborough Park attracts a variety of wildfowl

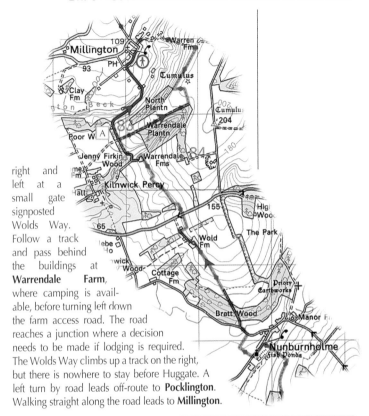

right and left at a small gate signposted Wolds Way. Follow a track and pass behind the buildings at **Warrendale Farm**, where camping is available, before turning left down the farm access road. The road reaches a junction where a decision needs to be made if lodging is required. The Wolds Way climbs up a track on the right, but there is nowhere to stay before Huggate. A left turn by road leads off-route to **Pocklington**. Walking straight along the road leads to **Millington**.

KILNWICK PERCY

Kilnwick Percy is slightly off-route, although some parkland and a substantial old hall might just be glimpsed. Kilnwick Percy Hall was first mentioned in the Domesday Book of 1086, though the present building is late-18th century. The estate fell on hard times and part of the hall was demolished, but the remainder has been restored as the Madhyamaka Buddhist Centre. Visits to the hall and gardens are available at certain times and there is a café on site.

Last view of the Wolds Way before moving off-route to the village of Millington

MILLINGTON

The little village of Millington has the Ramblers Rest pub, offering food and drink, while Laburnum Cottage offers bed-and-breakfast. Woldsbus links Millington with neighbouring Huggate, Pocklington, Nunburnholme and Market Weighton, along with distant Malton and Hull.

POCKLINGTON

The busy little market town of Pocklington lies 3km (2 miles) off-route, but has a good range of services if walkers need more than the basic facilities offered in the little wolds villages. It has a couple of hotels offering food, drink and accommodation, and there are banks with ATMs, a post office, plenty of pubs and restaurants, and lots of shops. East Yorkshire bus X46 runs regularly to York, Market Weighton, Beverley and Hull. Bus 199 is a Tuesday-only service to Nunburnholme and Huggate. Woldsbus offers links with the nearby towns and villages of Millington, Nunburnholme, Londesborough and Market Weighton, as well as distant Malton and Hull.

DAY 4
Millington to Thixendale

Start	Ramblers Rest, Millington, grid ref 831518
Finish	Cross Keys, Thixendale, grid ref 845610
Distance	23.5km (14.5 miles)
Maps	OS Landrangers 100 and 106, OS Explorers 294 and 300
Terrain	Several ascents and descents across wolds and dales, with some short, steep stretches early in the day. Easy roads, tracks and paths through cultivated fields for most of the rest of the time.
Refreshments	Huggate, Fridaythorpe and Thixendale each have pubs.
Public Transport	Woldsbus services link Pocklington, Huggate, Fridaythorpe and Thixendale, as well as more distant Malton and Hull. East Yorkshire bus 135 links Fridaythorpe with Great Driffield

This day's walk leads well into the heart of the Yorkshire Wolds, first by embarking on a roller-coaster route up and down the steep slopes of a few dales, then enjoying views across its huge field systems, along with the 'big sky' feeling of spaciousness. Huggate is the first village passed during the day's walk, and although just off-route most walkers are happy to detour the short distance, if only to visit the Wolds Inn. The village is in a remote setting, is quaint and charming, and provides basic services to wayfarers. Fridaythorpe is the next village and the route goes straight through it, but while it is interesting it is also on a busy main road and lacks a touch of solitude. At the end of the day Thixendale is a remarkable retreat, hidden in a veritable maze of grassy dales and an ideal place to spend the night. However, here in the heart of the wolds it is always best to book your bed in advance.

Retrace your steps along the road from **Millington** (though there is a public footpath that can be used to climb straight uphill to link with the Wolds Way) and turn left up a clear track, signposted the Wolds Way, climbing alongside **Warrendale Plantation**. The gradient eases at the top of the wood and you then turn left to walk straight across a field. Turn left downhill a short way, then right, to continue alongside a field with a view down to Millington, as well as further afield to Sutton Bank in the North York Moors and to the distant Pennines.

A tall hedgerow obscures views on the way towards **Warren Farm** where the farm access road is crossed. The Wolds Way continues alongside another field, following an old **earthwork** at around 190m (625ft). Swing left to descend alongside the field, then cross a stile and drop more steeply down into a grassy dale

Map continues p.50

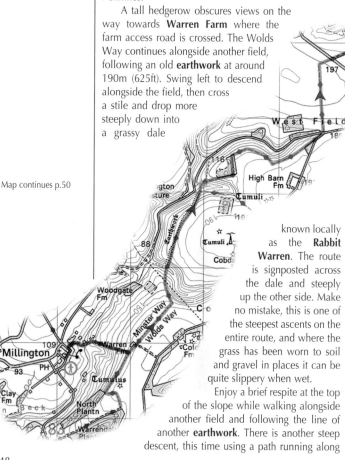

known locally as the **Rabbit Warren**. The route is signposted across the dale and steeply up the other side. Make no mistake, this is one of the steepest ascents on the entire route, and where the grass has been worn to soil and gravel in places it can be quite slippery when wet.

Enjoy a brief respite at the top of the slope while walking alongside another field and following the line of another **earthwork**. There is another steep descent, this time using a path running along

One of the steepest parts of the route involves crossing the Rabbit Warren

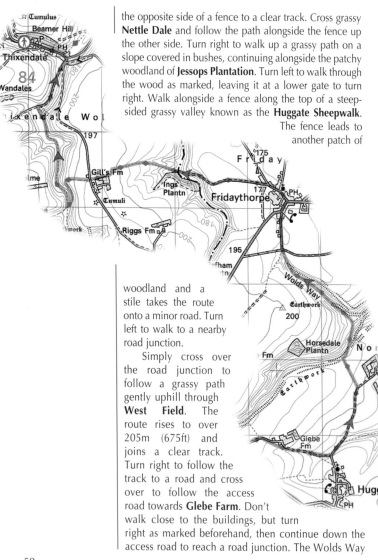

the opposite side of a fence to a clear track. Cross grassy **Nettle Dale** and follow the path alongside the fence up the other side. Turn right to walk up a grassy path on a slope covered in bushes, continuing alongside the patchy woodland of **Jessops Plantation**. Turn left to walk through the wood as marked, leaving it at a lower gate to turn right. Walk alongside a fence along the top of a steep-sided grassy valley known as the **Huggate Sheepwalk**. The fence leads to another patch of

woodland and a stile takes the route onto a minor road. Turn left to walk to a nearby road junction.

Simply cross over the road junction to follow a grassy path gently uphill through **West Field**. The route rises to over 205m (675ft) and joins a clear track. Turn right to follow the track to a road and cross over to follow the access road towards **Glebe Farm**. Don't walk close to the buildings, but turn right as marked beforehand, then continue down the access road to reach a road junction. The Wolds Way turns left here, but most walkers will be happy to turn right and go up through the lovely and peaceful village of **Huggate**.

HUGGATE

This delightful little village lies deep in the heart of the wolds and is a fine place to take a break. The whitewashed Wolds Inn, at 165m (540ft), offers food, drink and accommodation as well as camping, Manor House Farm, on the green, offers bed-and-breakfast, and there is a small post office with limited opening times that sells sweets and ice cream. Apart from those basic facilities there are quaint corners to explore. Woldsbus services link the village with Fridaythorpe and Millington, as well as distant Malton and Hull. There is also East Yorkshire bus 199, a Tuesday-only link with Pocklington.

Walk down the road away from **Huggate**, then gently uphill and along a tree-lined avenue with neatly mown edges that leads towards **Northfield House**. Turn left before reaching the house, as signposted alongside a field, at around 165m (540ft). Go through a small gate in a hedge and drift right to follow a path down the flank of an attractive grassy dale. The path slices across an ancient **earthwork** on its way to the floor of **Horse Dale**. Cross a stile over a fence at the bottom and turn left to walk up along the grassy floor of **Holm Dale**. Towards the top of the dale, branch right up a smaller dale and cross a stile at the

Walkers climb up through grassy Holm Dale on their way to Fridaythorpe

top to reach a track in a patch of woodland. Turn right to follow the track, which becomes a narrow road leading to the main A166 into the village of **Fridaythorpe** (a house on the corner is actually called **Wolds Way**). Turn right to follow the main road into the village, then left at the Manor House Inn to reach a quiet green and duck pond.

FRIDAYTHORPE

Fridaythorpe sits astride a busy road but has some quaint corners worth discovering. The box-like church, while being of no great antiquity, was built on a Norman foundation. A notice on the green near the duck pond marks the halfway point of the Wolds Way, as well as celebrating the 21st anniversary of the route and recording its re-launch in 2004 as the Yorkshire Wolds Way. The Wolds Way was first declared open on this very green.

Facilities include the Manor House Inn, offering food, drink and lodging, and there is also a butcher/baker in the village and a food store at a garage. East Yorkshire bus 135 runs to the nearby town of Great Driffield. Woldsbus services operate to neighbouring Thixendale and Huggate, as well as other Wolds Way villages and more distant Malton and Hull.

Follow the minor road from the green out of **Fridaythorpe** to pass the **ABN Feed Mill**. A track runs alongside the mill and the Wolds Way continues alongside a field. Cross a stile and follow a clear path slicing down across a steep and grassy slope into a dale, and continue past **Ings Plantation**. Cross another stile and turn left to walk up through a smaller dale, reaching a track at a higher level. Continue along the track, turning left only for a short way, then right and straight ahead again to walk alongside the trees surrounding **Gill's Farm**. Cross over a minor road at around 210m (690ft).

The Wolds Way runs straight onwards then turns left to follow a clear track that slices straight down across a steep grassy slope into a long dale. Turn sharp right at the bottom of the slope to walk down through the dale, which bends left and right. The grassy floor of the dale and a clear track lead to a road where the

Wolds Way is signposted to the right. The road runs through a dale cut deep into **Thixendale Wold** and walkers keep left at road junctions to enter the straggly village of **Thixendale** near the Cross Keys.

A Thixendale building that has been both a village school and a hostel

THIXENDALE

It has been suggested that originally this place name meant 'six dales' or even 'sixteen dales'. One thing is certain: a confusing maze of steep-sided grassy dales branches outwards from the village. Since land suitable for extensive ploughing and planting is so limited the area is largely given over to sheep rearing rather than cultivation

Facilities in Thixendale include the Cross Keys, a pub offering food, drink and accommodation, Manor Farm, providing bed-and-breakfast, and a post office shop and a shop with a café. Woldsbus services link with other villages along the Wolds Way such as Huggate and Wharram le Street, as well as more distant Hull and Malton.

53

DAY 5
Thixendale to Sherburn

Start	Cross Keys, Thixendale, grid ref 842611
Finish	Sherburn, grid ref 958767
Distance	29km (18 miles)
Maps	OS Landrangers 100 and 101, OS Explorer 300
Terrain	Easy roads, tracks and paths throughout the day, but several ascents and descents across wolds and dales, with some short, steep slopes.
Refreshments	None actually on the route, but a short distance off-route Wolds Way Lavender Farm has a café and North Grimston has a pub. There is a pub, restaurant and takeaway at Sherburn.
Public Transport	Woldsbus services pass through Wharram le Street and Wintringham on their way between Malton and Hull. The Moorsbus service also passes through Wharram le Street, linking Hull and Beverley with Malton and Thornton-le-Dale. A Postbus links Wharram le Street with Malton, except Sunday. Yorkshire Coastliner bus 843 links West Heslerton, East Heslerton and Sherburn with Ganton and Scarborough, as well as Malton, York and Leeds. Coastliner bus 845 runs through all three villages to Leeds and Filey.

The route remains very much in the heart of the Yorkshire Wolds, wandering through the dales, in and out of woodlands and traversing huge field systems. A highlight of the day is the deserted village of Wharram Percy, which is worth as much time as you can spare in exploration. Only two other villages are passed, Wharram le Street and Wintringham, though neither provides food and drink. It is possible to move off-route to the village of North Grimston, which has a pub, or visit Wolds Way Lavender Farm near Wintringham, which has a café. Towards the end of the day, if Sherburn seems too far away, walkers can drop down off-route to West Heslerton or East Heslerton in search of food, drink, lodging, or a bus even further off-route. Again, book your bed in advance!

Walk all the way through the village of **Thixendale** almost as far as Manor Farm, but turn right up a chalky track beforehand, slicing up across the steep slopes of **Beamer Hill**. Don't approach the farm or buildings tucked away in the small woodland, but turn left as marked along a grassy path. Link with a track on the far side and follow it across **Cow Wold** at around 200m (655ft). Be sure to cross a stile and turn left along a path just inside a field – *don't* follow the track any further. The path turns right and drops down into a grassy dale.

Walk across the dale as marked and head straight uphill through a smaller dale to cross a stile at the top. Walk alongside a field and into a patch of woodland to reach a prominent junction of tracks at around 215m (705ft). Turn right as signposted Wolds Way and follow a clear track alongside the shelter belt woodland of **North Plantation**. The track runs along the top of a fine grassy dale. By keeping left later, the course of the Wolds Way stays on the brow overlooking the dale. A gradual descent along this brow is followed by a steeper descent on a grassy path to reach a **millpond** and picnic area beside the deserted village of **Wharram Percy**.

WHARRAM PERCY

Take time to study the noticeboards around the site of this famous medieval deserted village. Most people head straight for the ruins of St Martin's Church, which is the most obvious remnant of the village, and thereby miss the outlines of several ancient dwellings on the higher grassy slopes. There are traces of prehistoric and Roman occupation, while the original timber church was a 10th-century Saxon construction. The outline of the North Manor, South Manor and peasant farmsteads can be traced by referring to the noticeboards around the site. The only house still standing is relatively modern, but it was built on the site of an 18th-century farmstead. It is used by archaeologists working on the site. As for the church, it was in use until 1949, but was inconveniently located away from surrounding villages. The tower fell down in 1959 and the ruins have since been consolidated.

A restored millpond makes a picnic site at the deserted village of Wharram Percy

Follow the track away from **Wharram Percy** and turn right as marked to cross a little beck. A path climbs up a narrow, bushy valley to reach a car park by a road. Turn left along the road to pass **Bella House** and continue through fields. When the road suddenly turns right, walk straight ahead along a track beside a large field. Turn right along another road to walk into the village of **Wharram le Street**. Turn left at a crossroads to follow the B1248 down through the village.

WHARRAM LE STREET

There are few facilities in this little village, but some of the cottages are quite charmingly bedecked with flowers and the old church and school are worth searching for. There is a single bed-and-breakfast establishment, Red House. Woldsbus and Moorsbus services link with Hull and Malton, and there is also a Postbus service to Malton (not on Sundays).

Continue along the B1248 to leave **Wharram le Street**, then turn right up a clear track through fields to reach the B1253. This is known locally as **High Street** and runs to 171m (561ft). Cross it and continue along another track towards a building. Step to the left into a field and follow the boundary round to the left. Cross a stile and follow a fence along the top of another field at **The Peak**, then drop down to the right as sign-posted and cross a footbridge over tiny **Settrington Beck**. Walk up to a farm access road and turn right, though bear in mind that a left turn leads down to **North Grimston** and the chance to obtain food and drink at the village pub.

The access road leads up through a stable-yard at **Settrington Wood House**, climbing higher to reach a junction with a track. Turn right alongside a woodland, as signposted Wolds Way. Leave the track to follow a path along the edge of the wood, rising gradually uphill parallel to a track. Later, turn left to follow the track

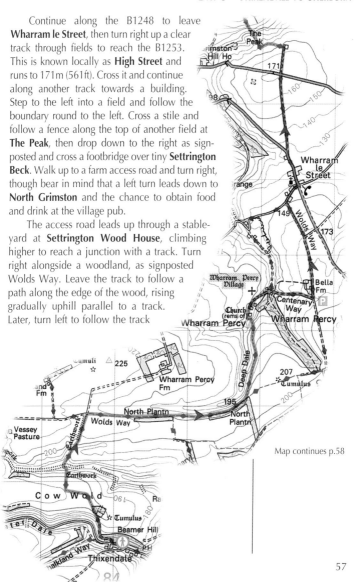

Map continues p.58

through the shelter belt woodland, then turn right to follow it gently uphill again. Another quick right and left turn leads through

Map continues p.60

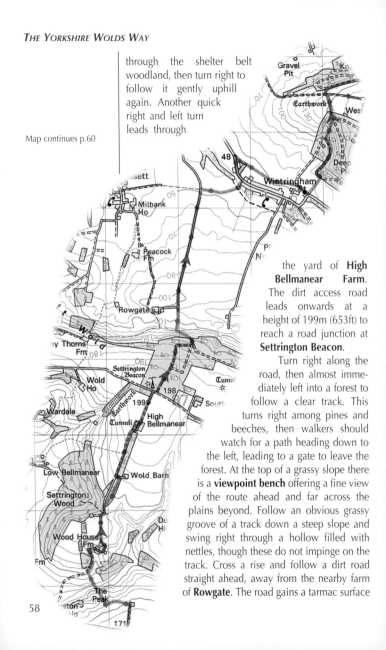

the yard of **High Bellmanear Farm**. The dirt access road leads onwards at a height of 199m (653ft) to reach a road junction at **Settrington Beacon**.

Turn right along the road, then almost immediately left into a forest to follow a clear track. This turns right among pines and beeches, then walkers should watch for a path heading down to the left, leading to a gate to leave the forest. At the top of a grassy slope there is a **viewpoint bench** offering a fine view of the route ahead and far across the plains beyond. Follow an obvious grassy groove of a track down a steep slope and swing right through a hollow filled with nettles, though these do not impinge on the track. Cross a rise and follow a dirt road straight ahead, away from the nearby farm of **Rowgate**. The road gains a tarmac surface

58

as it drops gently into a broad vale. Turn right as marked at the bottom, walking alongside a field and straight across another field. Cross a footbridge over **Wintringham Beck** and pass an attractive pond on the way to a road in the village of **Wintringham**.

WINTRINGHAM

There are several pretty cottages in Wintringham and the parish church is full of interest and well worth a visit, but there are no facilities for passing walkers. However, nearby Wolds Way Lavender Farm has a café on site offering food and drink. Lawns Travel operates an occasional bus to Malton, and Woldsbus services also link with nearby Malton, as well as with several Wolds Way villages all the way to distant Hull.

The parish church in Wintringham is a prominent landmark on the Wolds Way

Turn left along the road to leave **Wintringham**, then sharp right along a track known locally as **Back Side** that skirts the village alongside fields and almost reaches **Wintringham Church** at the other end of the village. Turn left here, away from the church, along a field path to reach a track. Turn left along this track and follow it across the foot of a wooded slope. Swing right and climb up through **Deepdale Plantation**, which has a mixture of beech and pines, and leave the upper part of the wood to continue along a path on top of an ancient **earthwork** flanked by bushes. Cross an access road signposted Wolds Way, walking straight towards **Knapton Plantation**. Follow a clear path to the right, just inside the plantation, and later leave it to cross a grassy gap where a small valley cuts the wooded brow. The route continues alongside another woodland on **West Heslerton Brow**, and later turns right to run parallel to a minor road before suddenly turning left to cross it. Bear in mind that this road could be followed downhill and off-route to the village of **West Heslerton**.

Staying on the Wolds Way, follow a gravel track alongside a small woodland and turn left around its boundary, then turn right to walk along grassy **East Heslerton Brow** to around 180m (590ft). Views across the Vale of Pickering extend to the North York Moors and the coast. Watch for another quick left and right turn later, and continue walking alongside a fence. Keep to the left of the woodland that surrounds **Manor Wold Farm** and hides it from view, but cross over the farm access road. Bear in mind that this road offers the chance to descend off-route to the village of **East Heslerton** in search of lodgings.

WEST AND EAST HESLERTON

These two little villages lie downhill from the Wolds Way. Most walkers don't visit them, but they offer handy facilities depending on your walking schedule. West Heslerton offers a guesthouse, post office and an inn serving food and drink. East Heslerton has a couple of bed-and-breakfast options and a fine church. Both villages are on Yorkshire Coastliner bus 843 and 845 routes, connecting with Scarborough and Filey respectively. Both bus routes link the two villages with Sherburn and Ganton, as well as Malton, York and Leeds.

Continue along East Heslerton Brow, crossing a field away from **Manor Wold Farm**. Follow a grassy track alongside a hedge and a wood, then turn left a short way

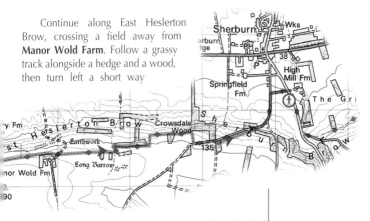

downhill and right to walk alongside a **coniferous plantation**. Notice the two graves in the corner at the far end of this plantation and watch for the Wolds Way heading downhill for a while. Turn right as signposted, and although the path is vague it basically follows a line of trees across the wooded slope, no doubt the remains of an ancient hedgerow. Turn right steeply uphill from **Crowsdale Wood**, levelling out at another patch of woodland beside a road at around 150m (490ft).

Turn left to follow the road gently downhill to a junction at the top of **Sherburn Brow**. Watch for the Wolds Way running parallel to the road, across a wooded slope,

61

Flinty fields put to the plough high on the Yorkshire Wolds at Manor Wold Farm

then rejoining the road to continue downhill. The road is called **Whitegates** and it levels out as it leads off-route to the village of **Sherburn**. Walkers who wish to stay on the Wolds Way should turn right along a clear track that simply runs from one road to another, though most will be happy to visit the village because of its services.

SHERBURN

Sherburn appeals because it provides a small range of services in an area largely bereft of food, drink and lodgings. St Hilda's Church is also interesting, with its Norman tower and examples of Saxon statuary.

Facilities include a bed-and-breakfast, post office store, pub, restaurant, takeaway and shop. Yorkshire Coastliner bus 843 runs from Leeds to Scarborough, linking the village with West and East Heslerton and nearby Ganton. Yorkshire Coastliner bus 845 runs to the same villages from Leeds and Filey. There is no station on the nearby railway.

DAY 6
Sherburn to Filey

Start	Sherburn, grid ref 958767
Finish	Filey Brigg, grid ref 126816
Distance	23.5km (14.5 miles)
Maps	OS Landranger 101, OS Explorers 300 and 301
Terrain	Mostly gentle field paths, farm tracks and quiet roads, though there are some short, steep descents and ascents while cross ing a few dales.
Refreshments	Ganton and Muston each have a single pub. Plenty of pubs, restaurants, cafés and takeaways around Filey.
Public Transport	Yorkshire Coastliner bus 845 links Ganton with Filey and Sherburn, on the way to York and Leeds. East Yorkshire bus 121 links Filey with Muston, as well as running all the way back to Hull. Arriva trains run from Filey to Scarborough and back to Hull.

The Wolds Way leaves Sherburn and stays fairly low on the slopes through Potter Brompton and Ganton, then climbs high and sails over the top of Staxton Wold. Several small grassy dales are crossed, or followed, before the route finally descends from the high ground. The little village of Muston is followed by the busy seaside resort of Filey, a place that hardly seems to have anything in common with the Yorkshire Wolds. Essentially the walk is over, and all that remains is the short stretch out onto the crumbling clay promontory of Filey Brigg. However, walkers who wish to keep going can follow the Cleveland Way along the coast to Scarborough, which is offered as an extra day's walk, so that the route comfortably fills the week.

Walkers leaving **Sherburn** find themselves at a fork in the road. To the right is **Whitegates**, the road that was followed into the village the previous day. To follow every part of the Wolds Way walkers should go back up this road and turn left along a clear track. However, if they take the other fork they will rejoin the Wolds Way where the track reaches the road not far from **High Mill**. Either way, continue along the road up to another fork and turn left. Another left turn reveals a path running across a slope of grassy areas and patchy woodlands. Follow the route as signposted across the slope, sometimes without any views if the woods on either side are particularly dense. Turn right uphill later, then left at a small gate to walk back down a woodland path.

Emerging from the wood, walk down through fields and turn right, soon passing the end of a coniferous shelter belt. Continue along the track through the fields to reach some attractive buildings in the little farming hamlet of **Potter Brompton**. Turn right along a road, then almost immediately left along a clear track running alongside more fields at the foot of the slope. Turn left down a minor road, away from **Ganton Hall** and its extensive grounds. Turn right at a junction to walk alongside the village of **Ganton**, keeping right of St Nicholas' Church and its 14th-century spire.

An attractive old stone building in the farming hamlet of Potter Brompton

GANTON

Facilities at Ganton are limited to the Ganton Greyhound Inn down on the main road, offering food, drink and accommodation. Yorkshire Coastliner bus 843 on the main road links with Scarborough, Sherburn, Malton, York and Leeds, while Yorkshire Coastliner bus 845 links with Filey and Leeds.

Follow a field path straight away from **St Nicholas' Church** and go through a gap in a shelter belt woodland. Turn right uphill until a left turn is marked alongside a field. This leads to a clear track called **Wold Lane**, which is followed to the right, straight uphill, narrowing as it approaches **Binnington Brow**. Turn left as marked at the corner of a field, then later turn right over a stile to walk alongside another field. Turn left again over another stile and walk alongside another field to reach the busy B1249 at **Staxton Wold Farm**. Cross over the road and continue straight onwards as signposted along a quiet minor road. This leads to the military installation of **RAF Staxton Wold**, where walkers turn right and pass alongside the security fence at 178m (504ft).

Map continues p.66

The road becomes a track as it leaves **RAF Staxton Wold** and drops down into a small wooded dale. Towards the bottom watch for a turning on the left, steeply uphill alongside a fence. The gradient

RAF STAXTON WOLD

This military installation seems incongruous in the peaceful wolds, but it is one of a number of early warning stations located throughout eastern England. It was built in 1939, just in time to monitor airborne activity during the Second World War. However, it was almost destroyed by the RAF themselves in 1942 when a Halifax bomber had to drop all its explosives near the site while executing an emergency landing because of a fire onboard. In the interests of security RAF Staxton Wold is not marked on any maps you can buy.

eases as the fence leads onwards alongside fields. Turn right around a corner of the field then turn left to walk alongside another field. Drop down into a small grassy dale, climb up the other side, then cross a smaller dale. Cross the slopes of **Flixton Wold** and continue straight across larger **Lang Dale**. All these dales are likely to be used for sheep grazing, while all around are cultivated fields. Follow the line of a fence along the remains of an old hawthorn hedge to reach a minor road. Turn right to follow it over a rise above 150m (490ft).

Turn left to leave the road as signposted Wolds Way and walk along the brow of **Raven Dale**, following the line of a fence and ancient **earthwork**. There is

a short, steep descent and re-ascent across the head of **Camp Dale**, closely following the fence. Note the scrub woodland on the left that fills the head of the dale. Turn right and right again, then left, to get round another little dale-head, then follow an uncultivated strip of grass between large fields high on **Folkton Wold**. When a fence is reached the Wolds Way is signposted down to the right, crossing the fence at a lower level. Walk down along the floor of the dale to reach some rumpled earthworks at a confluence of dales. These earthworks are known as **The Camp**.

Turn left to walk up through **Stocking Dale**, where patchy scrub woodland covers the valley sides. Keep to the grassy floor of the dale until the marked route leaves it, then turn right to walk alongside a belt of woodland planted on top of a linear **earthwork**. Turn left along an uncomfortably stony track to pass **Stockendale Farm** and reach a minor road at almost 130m (425ft).

Cross over the road and walk along a track beside a shelter belt woodland close to **Muston Wold Farm**. Bear right as marked later, across a field then over a stile and down alongside more fields. This is the final descent as the Yorkshire Wolds

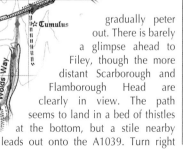

Map continues p.69

gradually peter out. There is barely a glimpse ahead to Filey, though the more distant Scarborough and Flamborough Head are clearly in view. The path seems to land in a bed of thistles at the bottom, but a stile nearby leads out onto the A1039. Turn right

Bright poppies grow profusely among the crops on the way to Stockendale Farm

along the road to reach the village of **Muston**. Walk through the village along West Street to pass the Ship Inn, continuing along King Street to pass All Saints Church.

MUSTON

Facilities are limited in this pretty little village, though the Yorkshire Wolds Way is rapidly coming to a close. The Ship Inn offers food and drink. East Yorkshire bus 121 runs regularly and daily to and from Filey, Scarborough, Bridlington and Hull.

On the way out of **Muston** watch for a Wolds Way signpost on the left, indicating a short field path that leads from the A1039 to the busier A165. Cross over the road and continue along another field path, turning left later close to a school **sports field**. Turn right along a grassy track between the sports field and some houses to reach the A1039 again. Turn left to follow this road – called Muston Road – into **Filey**.

The course of the Wolds Way through Filey isn't always clear, so keep an eye open for street names. **Muston Road** leads from the suburbs to a level crossing near the station where **Station Avenue** continues into town. Turn left along **Union Street** then right along **Mitford Street**. Turn left along **Reynolds Street** and right along **Queen Street** to reach the town council offices. Turn left along an alley that swings right and leads down a flight of steps to a toilet block. Across the road is the **Coble Landing**, where fishing boats are brought up from the beach (Coble is pronounced 'cobble').

Just inland from the **Coble Landing** walk up a zigzag path on a wooded slope and continue along the low, grassy cliff-top path. This passes above Filey Sailing Club, then a flight of steps leads into little **Wool Dale** and up the other side. Continue along the grassy cliff path through **Filey Country Park** and walk out onto the crest of **Filey Brigg** to

69

enjoy the sea breeze. Nearby a stone sculpture carved with the names of highlights from both routes commemorates the Yorkshire Wolds Way and Cleveland Way. At some point you have to decide whether to walk back into **Filey** or continue along the Cleveland Way and head towards the North York Moors National Park.

FILEY BRIGG

The grassy top of Filey Brigg has been crumbling steadily over the centuries and will one day be gone, leaving only the hard calcareous gritstone bedrock beneath. A Roman signal station and 12th-century castle have already been lost as the clay cliffs gradually crumble, and walkers are now forbidden to continue along the badly worn clay ridge leading down to the rocky slabs of Brigg End. If you want to walk to the very end of the Brigg you should do it by walking along Filey Sands when the tide is out, but bear in mind that the rocks are covered in slippery seaweed and big waves break across them without warning. There is an emergency telephone for those who find themselves marooned out on the point or spot anyone in obvious difficulty or danger.

FILEY

Filey is a little fishing town that has turned its attention to tourism. On the Coble Landing fishing boats lie on trailers beside amusement arcades, as if the transition is not yet complete. The town is fairly small yet supports a good variety of services, whether walkers are at the end of the Yorkshire Wolds Way or about to begin the Cleveland Way.

Facilities include a range of accommodation and a nearby campsite. There are banks with ATMs, a post office, toilets, plenty of pubs, restaurants, cafés and takeaways, as well as shops. The museum should be visited by anyone wanting a potted history of the town. There is a tourist information centre on John Street, tel 01723 518000. East Yorkshire bus 121 runs to Scarborough as well as back to Muston and distant Hull, and bus 120 also runs between Filey and Scarborough. Yorkshire Coastliner bus 845 links Filey with York and Leeds, passing the Wolds Way villages of Ganton, Sherburn and East and West Heslerton. Arriva trains run from Filey to Scarborough as well as back to Hull.

DAY 7
Filey to Scalby Mills
(via the Cleveland Way)

Start	Coble Landing, Filey, grid ref 120809
Finish	Sea Life Centre, Scalby Mills, grid ref 035907
Distance	19km (12 miles)
Maps	OS Landranger 101, OS Explorer 301
Terrain	Straightforward cliff coast walking leads to a rugged wooded slope, then urban walking along streets, roads and promenades to the end.
Refreshments	Beach hut and surf shop at Cayton Bay. Plenty of pubs, restaurants, cafés and takeaways around Scarborough.
Public Transport	Scarborough & District bus services run all around Scarborough, while East Yorkshire buses 120 and 121 operate between Filey and Scarborough. Arriva trains run between Filey and Scarborough.

For those who wish to extend their walk along the Yorkshire Wolds Way, part of the Cleveland Way is offered in reverse. This is a fine one-day coastal walk in its own right, but it also offers the chance to join the Link through the Tabular Hills Walk and the main circuit of the Cleveland Way all in one long journey. Of course walkers who use this guidebook simply to follow the Cleveland Way will also find this day's walk described from Scarborough to Filey, the way most walkers cover it at the end of the Cleveland Way. The route is fairly straightforward, but bear in mind that it is not marked or signposted through Scarborough, though there are a couple of suggestions for negotiating a way through the town. The route is described to Scalby Mills, just outside Scarborough, where walkers can immediately start walking along the Link.

Leave **Filey** from the road near the **Coble Landing**, where fishing boats are brought up from the beach. Just a short

Take care if venturing out onto the slippery, tidal, rocky reef of Filey Brigg

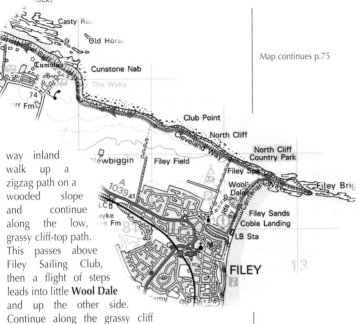

Map continues p.75

way inland walk up a zigzag path on a wooded slope and continue along the low, grassy cliff-top path. This passes above Filey Sailing Club, then a flight of steps leads into little **Wool Dale** and up the other side. Continue along the grassy cliff path through **Filey Country Park** and walk out onto the crest of **Filey Brigg**. Nearby a stone sculpture commemorating the Yorkshire Wolds Way and the Cleveland Way is carved with the names of highlights from both routes.

Continue walking along the cliff path and you pass an unremarkable field boundary that is technically where the Yorkshire Wolds Way and Cleveland Way meet, though nothing announces this fact to passers-by. Follow the easy, grassy cliff path along **Newbiggin Cliff** and turn around **Cunstone Nab**. Pass a caravan site while heading gently downhill along **Gristhorpe Cliff**, then turn around another headland, enjoying fine views ahead to Scarborough. The path climbs over the top of **Lebberston Cliff**, reaching 80m (260ft) above sea level, then descends and runs seawards of a row of houses and a cliff-top cottage. Between the houses and cottage there is access inland to a **surf shop** that sells sweets and ice cream.

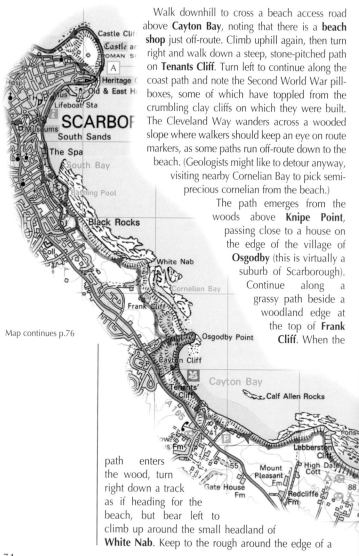

Walk downhill to cross a beach access road above **Cayton Bay**, noting that there is a **beach shop** just off-route. Climb uphill again, then turn right and walk down a steep, stone-pitched path on **Tenants Cliff**. Turn left to continue along the coast path and note the Second World War pill-boxes, some of which have toppled from the crumbling clay cliffs on which they were built. The Cleveland Way wanders across a wooded slope where walkers should keep an eye on route markers, as some paths run off-route down to the beach. (Geologists might like to detour anyway, visiting nearby Cornelian Bay to pick semi-precious cornelian from the beach.)

The path emerges from the woods above **Knipe Point**, passing close to a house on the edge of the village of **Osgodby** (this is virtually a suburb of Scarborough). Continue along a grassy path beside a woodland edge at the top of **Frank Cliff**. When the

Map continues p.76

path enters the wood, turn right down a track as if heading for the beach, but bear left to climb up around the small headland of **White Nab**. Keep to the rough around the edge of a

The sandy sweep of Cayton Bay is barely glimpsed from the wooded slopes

THE HOLBECK LANDSLIDE

The Holbeck Hall Hotel was built as a private residence in 1880 and later converted into a hotel. Unfortunately the ground beneath the building was essentially unstable and began to slump on 3 June 1993, an event that was documented as it happened by TV crews. The following day the hotel was in ruins and about a million tonnes of material had slumped into the sea in a huge bulge. An information board beside the Sea Cliff Road car park shows before and after pictures of the event, and the area has since been landscaped.

golf course, close to a crumbling clay cliff that displays numerous landslips. The path later runs across a wooded slope and emerges just below a car park at the end of **Sea Cliff Road**. The Holbeck Hall Hotel once stood nearby.

There is no waymarked route for the Cleveland Way through **Scarborough**. Walkers could follow the clear track down to the sea and head straight for town via the **Spa Complex** at South Bay, but be warned that the coastal path can be completely overwhelmed in heavy seas and in such conditions is not considered safe to follow. For a safe alternative follow **Sea Cliff Road** inland and turn right and right again to reach **Holbeck Hill**, which leads on to the **Esplanade** near a monumental clock and pleasure gardens. Signposts point into a network of interesting paths that crisscross **South Cliff** to reach the **Spa Complex** at South Bay.

Some writers say that wayfarers should avoid walking through Scarborough, even suggesting that they take one of the open-top buses from the Spa Complex at South Bay to the Corner Café at North Bay, but this seems unfortunate, given that the town abounds in interest, history and heritage. One easy option would be to walk along the promenade, along **Foreshore Road** to the harbour, then along **Marine Road** and around the headland, finally going along **Royal Albert Drive** to the **Corner Café**.

A more interesting approach is as follows: leave the **Spa Complex** and walk around South Bay using **Foreshore Road**. (To visit the town centre, use one of the cliff lifts or walk up the steep road called Blands Cliff.) At the far side of the **Old Harbour** turn left up **Castlegate**, as signposted, to reach **Scarborough Castle** on top of the headland.

SCARBOROUGH CASTLE

Bronze Age settlers are though to have been the first to fortify the headland at Scarborough. The Romans operated a signal station on a line of sight linked with other coastal signal stations at Ravenscar and Filey Brigg. In the 12th century Scarborough Castle was built on the headland. The castle withstood a 20-day siege during the Pilgrimage of Grace in 1536, but surrendered after a year-long siege during the Civil War in 1645. The ruins of the castle can be visited while exploring the town (there is an entrance charge).

SCARBOROUGH

The emergence of Scarborough as a premier holiday resort can be traced to the promotion of its spa waters. In 1626 a local doctor extolled the benefits of drinking the water, making so many claims about its curative properties that one must suspect quackery! However, visitors flocked to the town and before long the benefits of sea air and sea bathing were also being promoted. So enthusiastic were the crowds of holidaymakers that more and more facilities had to be built to cater for them. The arrival of the railway in 1845 boosted the tourism trade and the town remains a busy and bustling place to this day.

Facilities around Scarborough include a wide range of accommodation options, from splendid hotels to humble bed-and-breakfasts, as well as a youth hostel at Scalby Mills and nearby campsites. There are banks with ATMs, post offices, toilets, and an abundance of pubs, restaurants, cafés and takeaways to suit all tastes, though in many cases it's 'chips with everything'. As a shopping centre Scarborough has the greatest choice of any place visited in this guidebook. There is a tourist information centre opposite the railway station, tel 01723 373333. Trains run to a number of destinations throughout the country and there are Arriva trains to Filey and Hull. Yorkshire Coastliner bus 843 links Scarborough with York and Leeds. Arriva bus 93 runs to Robin Hood's Bay, Whitby, Guisborough and Middlesbrough. Scarborough & District bus 3A runs daily except Sunday from the Sea Life Centre to Scarborough. East Yorkshire buses 120 and 121 run from Scarborough to Filey, and there are plenty of other buses operating all around town, including the open-top summer buses from North Bay to South Bay.

Leaving the castle, pass **St Mary's Church**, where the grave of novelist Anne Brontë is an attraction, turn right to reach cliff-top **Norbreck Hotel,** then turn left to walk along the top of the slope where hotels enjoy views of North Bay. Approaching the **Clifton** at the end of **Queens Parade**, drop down any of the paths and walk towards the **Corner Café** on the promenade. All that remains is a short walk along the traffic-free promenade to the Sea Life Centre at **Scalby Mills**. At this point walkers have immediate access to the Tabular Hills Walk, which converts the rest of the Cleveland Way into an enormous circular walk leading back to this point.

Farwath, where teas are offered at a ford close
to the North York Moors Railway (Day 2)

THE TABULAR HILLS WALK

The Tabular Hills stretch along the southern part of the North York Moors National Park. The land rises gently from south to north and is cut by a series of dales that leave tabular, or 'table-like', uplands between them. The gentle slope often ends abruptly at its northern end in a series of shapely knolls, or 'nabs', that look out towards the rolling moorlands at the heart of the national park.

The rocks making up the Tabular Hills belong to the Middle Oolite group in the Corallian series of the Jurassic period and are hence around 170 million years old. They are essentially a limestone and lime-rich sandstone series, porous enough to allow surface water to drain away rapidly, and seldom exposed. In the more deeply cut dales the bedrock is the older Oxford Clay, which is impervious and supports the flow of rivers and streams. While some parts of the Tabular Hills have been turned over to commercial forestry, the land is very fertile and easily ploughed. The soil is often too thin to support good root crops, but grain crops such as wheat, barley and oats are grown in rotation, rustling in the wind, and oilseed rape crops blaze yellow early in summer.

A view from Levisham Moor and Saltergate into the heart of the North York Moors (Day 1)

The Tabular Hills Walk leaves the wooded Ash Dale and crosses fields to reach Helmsley (Day 3)

The idea for creating a link between Scalby Mills and Helmsley to convert the enormous loop of the Cleveland Way into a circular walk originated in 1974. The route was worked out by Malcolm Boyes, and he and several others walked the route, which they called the Missing Link, in 1975.

The Tabular Hills Walk seeks to achieve the same thing, and although the course of this route differs in places, the main villages visited by both are the same. Walkers can either start with the Tabular Hills Walk and continue along the Cleveland Way, or walk the Cleveland Way first and complete a full circuit by following the Tabular Hills Walk afterwards. Signposts and waymarks for the Tabular Hills Walk feature a directional arrow and a 'Tabular Hills' logo. The route has been designated a regional trail and is an initiative of the North York Moors National Park Authority.

DAY 1
Scalby Mills to Levisham

Start	Sea Life Centre, Scalby Mills, grid ref 035907
Finish	Horseshoe Inn, Levisham, grid ref 833906
Distance	34km (21 miles)
Maps	OS Landrangers 94, 100 and 101, OS Explorer OL27
Terrain	Generally easy paths, tracks and minor roads through fields and forest, ending with a moorland walk.
Refreshments	Pub at the start, pubs in Scalby, hotel at Eversley and a pub at Levisham.
Public Transport	Scarborough & District bus 3A runs daily except Sunday from Scarborough to the Sea Life Centre. Buses 12 and 21 run past Scalby Mills twice a day on Monday, Wednesday and Thursday. Bus 15 runs daily except Sunday from Scarborough to Scalby. Bus 16 serves Scalby from Scarborough and Ravenscar daily except Sunday. Yorkshire Coastliner bus 840 serves Saltergate Bank daily from Whitby and Malton.

Technically the Tabular Hills Walk begins where a footpath cuts inland from the coastal Cleveland Way to the village of Scalby Mills. Scalby Mills Youth Hostel makes a good starting point, but by setting off from Scarborough's Sea Life Centre walkers can follow a short stretch of coastal path before heading inland, with no need to double back on themselves. Bear in mind that facilities are limited throughout this day and the full distance to Levisham may not be within the capability of all walkers. If intermediate accommodation is needed there is a farmhouse bed-and-breakfast at Givendale Head, halfway through the day. (As always, book in advance if you plan to stay here.)

Start on the crumbling cliff coast just north of Scalby Mills where the Tabular Hills Walk branches off from the course of the Cleveland Way. While this junction of paths can be reached easily from the busy Burniston Road north of Scalby Mills, a much better approach is from the Sea Life Centre.

Alighting from the bus at the **Sea Life Centre** cross the footbridge over Scalby Beck beside the **Old Scalby Mills** pub and restaurant. Steps reveal the coastal path running northwards around **Scalby Ness**. Don't be tempted inland too early along a path overlooking the valley of **Scalby Beck**, but continue further along the coast path. The path running inland at the start of the Tabular Hills Walk is signposted Footpath to Burniston Road. Follow it through two fields to reach the busy A165 **Burniston Road** and turn right. (Scalby Mills Youth Hostel is a short distance left down the road.) Turn left along Field Lane, passing the entrance to the Scarborough Camping and Caravanning Club Site. Field Lane becomes Station Road as it enters **Scalby**, though the railway through the village operated only from 1885 to 1965. When the busy A171 **Scalby Road** is reached, either turn left to follow it downhill or walk straight along High Street if you wish to explore the centre of the village.

SCALBY

Facilities include a couple of shops and pubs, a café, post office and toilets. Regular Scarborough & District bus services run to and from Scarborough and Ravenscar (except Sunday).

Map continues p.85

THE SEA CUT

The River Derwent has its source on Fylingdales Moor, a mere spit and a throw from the North Sea. It flows towards the sea, but only 6km (4 miles) short of it suddenly swings west and heads far inland. Its waters eventually spill into the North Sea via the Humber Estuary after a circuitous journey of 240km (150 miles). The Sea Cut was engineered by the distinguished inventor Sir George Cayley (a pioneer in the science of aerodynamics, amongst other things) in the early 18th century. It diverts the headwaters of the River Derwent into Scalby Beck, passing floodwater straight to the sea instead of allowing it to inundate the Vale of Pickering. The Sea Cut also provided a good head of water for industry at Scalby Mills.

Walk down the busy main road only to cross **Scalby Beck**, then turn right alongside it using a grassy path. The river has obviously been artificially cut through the landscape and is flanked by earth embankments. The **Sea Cut**, as it is known, looks rather like a canal with a towpath.

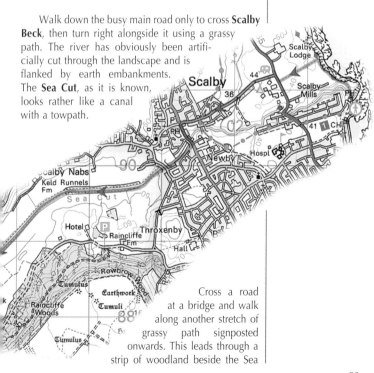

Cross a road at a bridge and walk along another stretch of grassy path signposted onwards. This leads through a strip of woodland beside the Sea

Map continues p.86

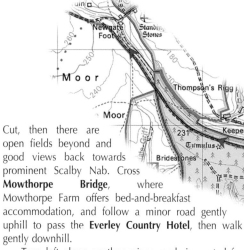

Cut, then there are open fields beyond and good views back towards prominent Scalby Nab. Cross **Mowthorpe Bridge**, where Mowthorpe Farm offers bed-and-breakfast accommodation, and follow a minor road gently uphill to pass the **Everley Country Hotel**, then walk gently downhill.

Turn left along another minor road signposted for **Wrench Green**. The road crosses the River Derwent, swinging right and left as it climbs through the hamlet. A steeper climb leads into woodlands, then the tarmac road levels out and proceeds as a gravel road into **Wykeham Forest**. Turn right at a junction then left at a fork to keep to the clearest gravel road, which is also waymarked as the Moors to Sea Cycleway. A viewpoint car park is reached at a junction with another narrow tarmac road at an altitude of 208m (682ft).

Walk straight along the road, passing a turning for the **Raptor Viewpoint** where birdwatchers may wish to make a brief detour. Fields alongside the road produce millions of tree seedlings every year, but just before reaching the entrance to the **Wykeham Forest Nursery** branch right along a clear track signposted the Link. Pass more tree plots and follow the track as it gradually descends to a narrow tarmac road near **Cockmoor Hall**. Take a moment to look at the rumpled ground on either side of the track, which are the ancient Cockmoor Dikes.

COCKMOOR DIKES

Over a dozen embankments and ditches run parallel at the Cockmoor Dikes, and a study of a detailed map reveals other ancient linear earthworks in the same area. These include the Scamridge Dikes and Oxmoor Dikes, thought to have been constructed by rival tribes to mark their territories.

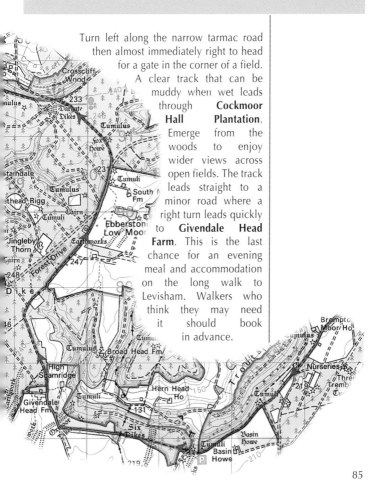

Turn left along the narrow tarmac road then almost immediately right to head for a gate in the corner of a field. A clear track that can be muddy when wet leads through **Cockmoor Hall Plantation**. Emerge from the woods to enjoy wider views across open fields. The track leads straight to a minor road where a right turn leads quickly to **Givendale Head Farm**. This is the last chance for an evening meal and accommodation on the long walk to Levisham. Walkers who think they may need it should book in advance.

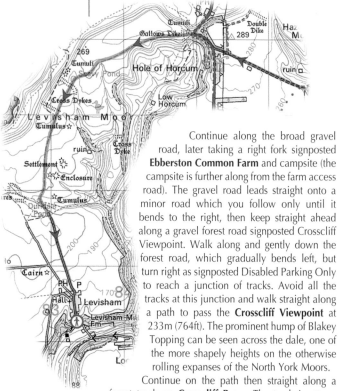

Continue along the broad gravel road, later taking a right fork signposted **Ebberston Common Farm** and campsite (the campsite is further along from the farm access road). The gravel road leads straight onto a minor road which you follow only until it bends to the right, then keep straight ahead along a gravel forest road signposted Crosscliff Viewpoint. Walk along and gently down the forest road, which gradually bends left, but turn right as signposted Disabled Parking Only to reach a junction of tracks. Avoid all the tracks at this junction and walk straight along a path to pass the **Crosscliff Viewpoint** at 233m (764ft). The prominent hump of Blakey Topping can be seen across the dale, one of the more shapely heights on the otherwise rolling expanses of the North York Moors.

Continue on the path then straight along a forest track on **Crosscliff Brow**. The track is attractively lined with deciduous trees that screen from view most of the nearby commercial conifers. There are occasional glimpses of Blakey Topping, then better views once the track goes through a gate and continues along grassy **Newgate Brow**. (Lying off-route to the south, but worth a visit, are the celebrated Bride Stones, where outcropping rock has been sculpted by the weather into bizarre forms.) At another gate join and follow uphill a tarmac farm access road – this is known as the Old Wife's Way and leads to the busy A169 on **Saltergate Brow**.

Cross the main road with care and turn right to follow a path overlooking the **Hole of Horcum**. The path runs parallel to the main road but safely away from the traffic. Poor, marshy fields seen below are flanked by bushy hedgerows and patchy woodlands, with heather moorland all around the head of the valley.

A long and straight track is followed on the way towards Givendale Head Farm

THE HOLE OF HORCUM

According to a locally favoured legend, a giant by the name of Wade was out of sorts with his wife and scooped up a pile of earth to throw at her. He missed, and the resulting hole became the Hole of Horcum while the lump of earth became Blakey Topping. The Saltergate Inn can be seen from a gap at the head of the Hole of Horcum and is easily visited if food and drink are required. Daily Yorkshire Coastliner bus 840 services pass Saltergate if walkers need to leave the route, offering links with Whitby, Lockton and Pickering.

Walkers follow a path around the Hole of Horcum, with the moors seen beyond

THE SALTERGATE INN

Saltergate was an important trading route running inland from the coast. It was also known as the Salt Road or Fish Road. Smugglers took illicit goods along it and were in the habit of holing up at the Saltergate Inn. According to local lore revenue men raided the place one night, but the smugglers ensured that nothing was discovered. However, one revenue man who lingered too long afterwards was killed and his body buried beneath the hearthstone of the inn. The landlord of the day insisted that a fire be kept continually ablaze to deter anyone from digging up the hearthstone, and this tradition was maintained for generations afterwards. The ever-blazing fire at the 'legendary Saltergate Inn' became a tourist attraction in its own right!

Follow a moorland track a short way uphill from the head of the Hole of Horcum and it soon levels out around 270m (885ft) on **Levisham Moor**. There is only one clear track across the undulating heather moorland, so route-finding errors are unlikely even though the area is quite featureless. Small cast-iron plaques mark features of interest along the way. Tiny **Seavy Pond** and **Dundale Pond**, dug in medieval times as watering-holes for livestock, might easily be passed unseen, choked as they are with vegetation. The track crosses a gap at the latter then forges uphill a short way to leave the moorland at a gate. The track becomes a tarmac road, **Limpsey Gate Lane**, leading down into the attractive and spacious village of **Levisham**.

LEVISHAM AND LOCKTON

Levisham has a broad central green surrounded by stout stone cottages and farmhouses. Facilities include the Horseshoe Inn for food, drink and accommodation, Rectory Farm House bed-and-breakfast, the Moorlands Country House, and a post office. There is a youth hostel at nearby Lockton, which also has a shop and tearoom. Yorkshire Coastliner bus 840 runs from Lockton to Saltergate, Whitby, Pickering, Malton and Leeds.

DAY 2
Levisham to Hutton-le-Hole

Start	Horseshoe Inn, Levisham, grid ref 833906
Finish	Ryedale Folk Museum, Hutton-le-Hole, 705900
Distance	25km (15.5 miles)
Maps	OS Landrangers 94 or 100, OS Explorers OL26 and OL27
Terrain	Muddy paths at first then mostly clear tracks and roads. Some short ascents and descents across wooded dales with large fields in between.
Refreshments	Teas at Farwath. Pubs at Newton-on-Rawcliffe, Cropton, Appleton-le-Moors and Hutton-le-Hole.
Public Transport	Moorsbus services link Newton-on-Rawcliffe, Keldy and Cropton with Thornton-le-Dale. Hutchinsons buses offer limited links between Newton-on-Rawcliffe and Cropton, as well as Appleton-le-Moors, Hutton-le-Hole and Kirkbymoorside. Hutton-le-Hole has regular Moorsbus services, linking with Pickering, Helmsley and Sutton Bank.

After the rather remote first day's walk this stage of the Link includes a succession of charming little villages, each one in turn featuring at least a pub offering food and drink, and there are also a couple of accommodation options. The route crosses the North York Moors Railway, where steam-hauled trains may be spotted. The railway and surrounding area features regularly in the popular television series Heartbeat. At the end of this stage the Ryedale Folk Museum at Hutton-le-Hole is well worth exploring. Over a dozen cottages, houses, farms and shops feature life throughout the ages in this part of Yorkshire, with plenty of supporting artefacts and implements on display.

Walk down through **Levisham** to pass the Moorlands Country House at the bottom end of the village. Follow a zigzag road steeply downhill and turn right along a track as signposted. The ruin of **St Mary's Church** lies down to the left, but keep straight ahead and walk along a path on the inside edge of a wood overlooking the ruined church in the valley.

LEVISHAM CHURCH

St Mary's Church, on an 11th-century foundation and tucked deep in a steep-sided valley, seems rather remote from Levisham village. According to legend it was supposed to be built in the village, but each night the Devil carried all the building materials down into the valley. The church was virtually abandoned before the tower was added, and a new church was built in 1884 at a more convenient location in the village.

The route varies from a muddy woodland track to a grassy path, passing through a succession of gates to reach a footbridge over **Levisham Beck**. The marshy grassland near the beck is the Hagg Wood Marsh nature reserve, where alkaline waters allow an interesting assemblage of plants to flourish. Turn right at **Farwath**, crossing the North York Moors Railway at a level crossing, and maybe take a break at the Farwath Tea Gardens.

The ruins of St Mary's Church lie deep in a valley below the village of Levisham

NORTH YORK MOORS RAILWAY

This scenic railway runs between Pickering and Grosmont, a distance of 29km (18 miles), and is famous for its steam-hauled services, though when it opened in 1836 the carriages were actually horse-drawn. The line was engineered by George Stephenson but had to be improved considerably before steam trains could use it. Although closed in 1964, it was subsequently re-opened by a group of dedicated railway enthusiasts and is now an immensely popular tourist attraction. Scenes involving the line feature regularly in period films and on television, including the long-running Heartbeat series. Trains do not stop at Farwath, but Levisham Station can be reached by walking down into wooded Newton Dale from the village of Newton-on-Rawcliffe.

Cross another bridge over **Pickering Beck** and follow clear, gravel Farwath Road uphill across a wooded slope. It emerges at a junction of battered farm access roads where a right turn leads past **Howlgate Farm**. Keep to the farm access road to pass **East Brow House** and reach the top end of **Newton-on-Rawcliffe**, close to a road at 190m (625ft).

Map continues p.95

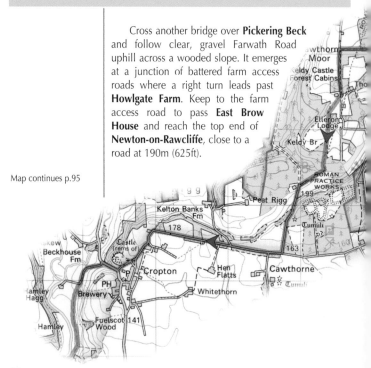

NEWTON-ON-RAWCLIFFE

The village features a splendid green with a duck pond surrounded by stone farmhouses and cottages. Facilities include a pub called the Mucky Duck offering accommodation, meals and a campsite. Other bed-and-breakfasts include Elm House Farm, Swan Cottage and Keld Farm. There are Moorsbus and Hutchinsons bus services to Cropton and Pickering.

Turn right at the top end of **Newton-on-Rawcliffe** without even touching the road if a visit to the village isn't needed. A track crosses a rise, then may be muddy for a short while before dropping down steep, wooded **Newton Banks** into a valley. Go through a gate and ford a beck, then follow a boulder-studded path up **Stony Moor**, where there is patchy woodland as well as heather and bilberry.

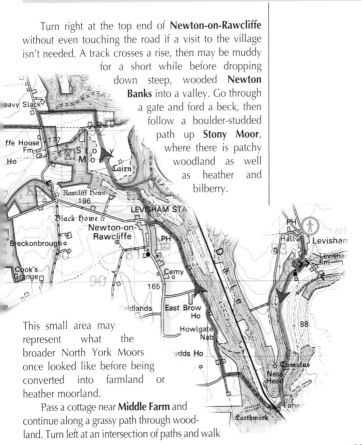

This small area may represent what the broader North York Moors once looked like before being converted into farmland or heather moorland.

Pass a cottage near **Middle Farm** and continue along a grassy path through woodland. Turn left at an intersection of paths and walk

93

straight ahead, out of the wood and through fields using a series of gates. Continue along a clear track to a road near **Seavy Slack** and turn left. Walk a short way down the road and turn right along a clear track known as the **Peat Road**, heading for **Cawthorn Moor** and touching 200m (655ft).

When a T-junction is reached, turn left to walk down a woodland track and go through a gate onto an access road. Turn right and left as indicated by signs for Keldy close together. Walk diagonally across a field, passing a solitary tree to reach a gate at the corner of a wood. Follow a clear path down through the wood and ford **Cold Keld Beck**. Turn right to follow a path uphill, then walk along the inside edge of the wood to reach a road and farm at **Keldy**. Turn left to follow the road uphill on a wooded slope where the rumpled earthworks of **Cawthorn Roman Camp** lie out of sight to the left.

CAWTHORN ROMAN CAMP

The Romans advanced rapidly through Britain during the first century AD, subduing the country by superior military might. They established a military practice camp on Cawthorn Moor, and the lack of any defensive works suggests that the local inhabitants were in no mood to attack the site.

Turn right after crossing the highest part of the road to follow **High Lane**. If you object to walking on tarmac, this road has broad grassy verges. The road reaches its highest point at **Bone Hill**, 178m (584ft), then descends and swings left down into the village of **Cropton**. The Link actually cuts off to the right just as High Farm bed-and-breakfast is reached.

Leave **Cropton** as signposted down a delightfully overgrown old lane passing **St Gregory's Church**. Turn right down a steep road, then left along a clear track as signposted for the Link. When the track suddenly turns right, leave it by walking straight ahead to enjoy a fine, garlic-scented woodland path along **Mill Bank**. Eventually, at a junction of paths turn right down to the **River Seven** and cross it using a footbridge. Follow

CROPTON

A motte and bailey was built at Cropton in the 12th century, but it was in ruins by the end of the 14th century. St Gregory's Church may have been built on a Norman chapel site, but while it retains its 12th-century font the building is essentially a 19th-century restoration.

Facilities in the village include the New Inn, offering accommodation, meals and tours of its thriving micro-brewery. Other accommodation includes Burr Bank, High Farm and Rose Cottage Farm bed-and-breakfasts. Moorsbus and Hutchinsons buses link with Newton-on-Rawcliffe and Pickering.

the nearby farm access road uphill, away from **Appleton Mill Farm**, and continue along Hamley Lane. Turn left at a road junction beside the stump of an old stone cross to approach **Appleton-le-Moors**. The route actually turns right just as it reaches **Dweldapilton Hall** on the outskirts of the village.

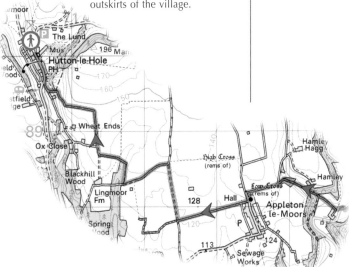

A pleasant track runs between fields as the route leaves Appleton-le-Moors

APPLETON-LE-MOORS

Appleton is a typical Yorkshire 'croft and toft' village. The crofts are the little cottages arranged on either side of the long main street, the tofts are the pieces of land extending out at the back of each dwelling where household-ers would grow their own vegetables. Imposing Dweldapilton Hall was built by a wealthy whaler. Facilities include the Moors Inn, offering food and accommodation, and Town End Farm bed-and-breakfast. Hutchinsons bus service offers limited links with Hutton-le-Hole, Gillamoor, Fadmoor, Kirkbymoorside and Pickering.

Follow the track away from the **hall**, passing the village **sports field** to reach a prominent junction of tracks. Turn right through a gate and follow an unenclosed track gently uphill through fields. Turn left along **Lingmoor Lane**, as signposted, at another prominent junction of tracks. Walk through a gate then into a wood at another gate. Turn right to walk around the inside edge of the wood, then continue through fields. Turn right along another clear track, **Bottomfields Lane**, rising gently. Turn left at the top and continue through more fields. The track then drops steep and narrow down to a road. Turn right to walk up into the charming village of **Hutton-le-Hole**.

HUTTON-LE-HOLE

Hutton-le-Hole has a long history of settlement dating back to Neolithic times. The village was mentioned in the Domesday Book as Hoton, and throughout the ages has also been rendered as Hege-Hoton, Hoton under Heg, and Hewton. As a place name Hutton-le-Hole dates only from the 19th century.

Facilities in this lovely village, which has a stream running through it, include the Ryedale Folk Museum, Barn Hotel, Moorlands Guest House, Crown Inn and a couple of tea shops. Moorsbus services link with Helmsley, Sutton Bank and Pickering, while Hutchinsons bus service offers limited links with Appleton-le-Moors, Pickering, Gillamoor, Fadmoor and Kirkbymoorside.

RYEDALE FOLK MUSEUM

Trace the history of Yorkshire folk from 4000BC to 1953, with plenty of hands-on exhibits, as you wander from one part of the museum site to another. Over a dozen buildings have been erected since 1964, some supported by enormous cruck frames (pairs of curved wooden timbers supporting the ends of the roof), many standing in isolation, while others are arranged as a row of small shops. Vintage vehicles, including motorised and horse-drawn carriages, are preserved, and land around the site sprouts vegetables and flowers, including many varieties of cornflowers. Local people often give demonstrations of traditional crafts while wearing period dress. There is an entrance charge, and the museum incorporates a shop, toilets and tourist information centre, tel 01751 417367.

Reconstructed shops and dwellings are a feature of the Ryedale Folk Museum

DAY 3
Hutton-le-Hole to Helmsley

Start	Ryedale Folk Museum, Hutton-le-Hole, grid ref 705900
Finish	Market cross, Helmsley, grid ref 613839
Distance	22km (13.5 miles)
Maps	OS Landrangers 94 or 100, OS Explorer OL26
Terrain	Mostly clear paths, tracks and roads crossing a succession of dales, fields and woodlands.
Refreshments	Pubs at Gillamoor and Fadmoor. Plenty of shops, pubs and restaurants around Helmsley.
Public Transport	Pickering, Helmsley and Sutton Bank. Hutchinsons buses offer limited links between Hutton-le-Hole, Cropton, Newton-on-Rawcliffe, Appleton-le-Moors and Kirkbymoorside, as well as buses to Gillamoor and Fadmoor. Helmsley is an important Moorsbus hub, with plenty of onward connections to points along the Cleveland Way. Scarborough & District bus 128 runs regularly through Helmsley to link with Sutton Bank, Kirkbymoorside, Pickering, Thornton-le-Dale and Scarborough.

The route crosses a succession of dales on its way from Hutton-le-Hole to Helmsley. A few of these are small and might barely be noticed, but others are larger and deeper, flanked by steep wooded slopes. A couple of charming little villages are passed, but for the most part the route is without facilities until the end of the day, and indeed the end of the route itself at Helmsley. At that point there is the widest range of services encountered on the whole route, as well as immediate access to the Cleveland Way for those hardy walkers who feel that their exploration of the North York Moors has only just commenced.

Follow the road uphill through **Hutton-le-Hole** and watch out for a public footpath signpost on the left. Follow a well-marked path through a succession of small fields to reach a little area of moorland. Follow only the waymarked path

downhill, avoiding all others, to cross a footbridge on the way towards **Grouse Hall**. Keep well to the left of the farm, walking through fields and down to the **River Dove**. Cross a footbridge and pass an old mill restored as a dwelling. The access road leads up to a wooded slope where it bends right. Turn left up a path signposted for the Link and emerge from the woods beside St Aidan's Church in **Gillamoor**, which has a fine viewpoint alongside. Walk straight through the village and continue along the road to reach the neighbouring village of **Fadmoor**.

Gillamoor is one of a series of charming farming villages passed by the Tabular Hills Walk

GILLAMOOR AND FADMOOR

These two charming little villages lacked a reliable water supply until the 18th century, when Joseph Foord engineered a lengthy aqueduct that tapped into distant sources of water and channelled a supply to the villages. This supply was still in use in the 20th century until it was replaced by piped water.

Facilities in Gillamoor include the Royal Oak Inn for food, drink and accommodation, as well as Manor Farm bed-and-breakfast and the Village Shop. Fadmoor has a spacious green and the Plough Inn offers food and drink. Both villages are on a Moorsbus route linking with Hutton-le-Hole and Helmsley. There are also limited Hutchinsons bus services to Hutton-le-Hole, Appleton-le-Moors, Pickering and Kirkbymoorside.

Turn left at the **Plough Inn** then right along a road signposted for Sleightholmedale. The road runs through fields, then another right turn leads along **Green Lane**, which has an avenue of trees alongside. Follow the road gently downhill then turn left along a track into **Mell Bank Wood**. The track later runs through fields then drops down a wooded slope. Keep left in the woods to reach a stone bridge at **Hold Caldron Mill**, deep in Kirk Dale.

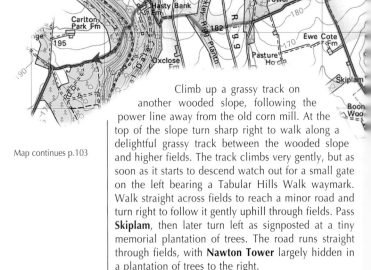

Map continues p.103

Climb up a grassy track on another wooded slope, following the power line away from the old corn mill. At the top of the slope turn sharp right to walk along a delightful grassy track between the wooded slope and higher fields. The track climbs very gently, but as soon as it starts to descend watch out for a small gate on the left bearing a Tabular Hills Walk waymark. Walk straight across fields to reach a minor road and turn right to follow it gently uphill through fields. Pass **Skiplam**, then later turn left as signposted at a tiny memorial plantation of trees. The road runs straight through fields, with **Nawton Tower** largely hidden in a plantation of trees to the right.

When a road junction is reached walk straight down a woodland path signposted as a bridleway. Cross the little valley of **Howldale** and climb up the other side to walk through fields. Cross a road on **Beadlam Rigg**, walk through fields and drop down into wooded **Pinderdale**. Follow the path uphill out of the valley and into the higher fields, and cross another

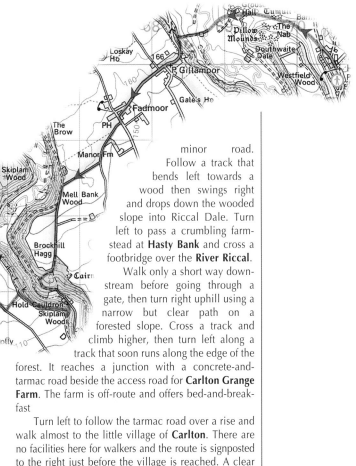

minor road. Follow a track that bends left towards a wood then swings right and drops down the wooded slope into Riccal Dale. Turn left to pass a crumbling farmstead at **Hasty Bank** and cross a footbridge over the **River Riccal**.

Walk only a short way downstream before going through a gate, then turn right uphill using a narrow but clear path on a forested slope. Cross a track and climb higher, then turn left along a track that soon runs along the edge of the forest. It reaches a junction with a concrete-and-tarmac road beside the access road for **Carlton Grange Farm**. The farm is off-route and offers bed-and-breakfast

Turn left to follow the tarmac road over a rise and walk almost to the little village of **Carlton**. There are no facilities here for walkers and the route is signposted to the right just before the village is reached. A clear gravel track called **Keld Lane** runs straight through fields before swinging right to drop down into **Ash Dale**. Turn left to follow a track along the grassy floor of the valley, with steep wooded slopes on either side. There is no way of gauging progress down-dale, but when the steep bank on the right dwindles to nothing

101

Old buildings lying deep in wooded Kirk Dale alongside Hold Caldron Mill

watch for a narrow path slipping out of the woods on that side. Walk alongside a field and through a gate. Turn right through fields to reach another gate, then turn left. Turn right round the field and left at another gate and walk into **Helmsley** via Warwick Place. Then either turn left along a road to reach the youth hostel, or right for All Saints Church, and then keep left to enter the Market Place and finish at the **market cross** – or prepare yourself to embark on the Cleveland Way.

HELMSLEY

Helmsley is a quintessential Yorkshire market town tracing its ancestry back to Anglo-Saxon times. The spacious Market Place fills with stalls on market day and serves as a car park at other times. Apart from the market cross there is a towering monument to the second Lord Feversham. Stout stone buildings stand on all sides of the Market Place, and a couple of poky alleys lined with quaint little shops lead away. The most prominent building is the Town Hall. All Saints Church is just outside the Market Place, founded in Norman times but essentially a 19th-century structure.

Helmsley is the largest town on the Tabular Hills Walk and offers the fullest range of facilities. There is a good range of accommodation, banks with ATMs, post office, toilets, plenty of pubs, restaurants and tearooms, as well as shops galore, including an outdoor gear store. The tourist information centre is in the Town Hall on Market Place, tel 01439 770173. There are plenty of buses through town: Scarborough & District bus 128 offers regular daily links to Sutton Bank and Scarborough, regular Moorsbus services head to places back along the route such as Fadmoor, Gillamoor and Hutton-le-Hole, as well as ahead along the Cleveland Way, including to Rievaulx, Sutton Bank and Clay Bank. Change onto other Moorsbus services to reach Lord Stones and Osmotherley.

Fine old shops and buildings are clustered around Helmsley's Market Place

HELMSLEY CASTLE

Not every visitor to Helmsley is aware of Helmsley Castle, despite its proximity to the town centre. It was built around 1200 and saw plenty of strife in 1644 during the Civil War. Colonel Crosland held the castle for the Crown, while Sir Thomas Fairfax led the besieging Parliamentarian force. Fairfax was hit by a musket ball during one assault and his siege was threatened by a Royalist force from Knaresborough Castle. This relief force was beaten back and harried as far as Black Hambleton, which might be construed as an early attempt to cover the Cleveland Way! The castle surrendered towards the end of 1644 and was rendered useless during 1646 and 1647 when parts of the keep and walls were destroyed. It can be visited for an entrance charge

THE CLEVELAND WAY NATIONAL TRAIL

The Cleveland Hills form the western slopes of the North York Moors National Park. The hills rise to no great height, with only a few exceeding 400m (1300ft), but all of them rise abruptly from the plains. Views from these hills are therefore of contrasting agricultural lowlands and wild, open heather moorlands in the heart of the North York Moors. These moorlands have long been man-managed in the interest of grouse shooting and represent the largest extent of heather moorland in the country. Views from the eastern cliff coastline also offer a contrast, this time between the open North Sea and the intricate agricultural landscape, cleft by wooded valleys and dotted with seaside resorts where fishing is giving way to tourism.

The rocks making up the Cleveland Hills and coast are generally from the lower and middle Jurassic periods, and are some 170–200 million years old. The lower beds include Lias shales and ironstones, which have been extensively quarried, whereas the higher moorlands are generally capped by sandstones from the Ravenscar group, although there are crumbling shale beds too. The sandstones effectively protect the lower rocks and determine the plateau-like structure of the North York Moors. To the southwest, around Helmsley and Osmotherley, the slightly younger rocks of the oolite group are exposed – more dramatically so than in the Tabular Hills. Much of the bedrock in the northeast and southeast of the area is buried beneath deep deposits of ill-sorted glacial drift and alluvium.

The Cleveland Way was the second national trail to be established in Britain (the Pennine Way was first) and was officially opened in 1969. The route was devised as a loop around the North York Moors National Park, starting from Helmsley and taking in the steep scarp slope overlooking the plains in the west, all the way to Guisborough, before hugging the cliff coast from Saltburn to Filey to the east. The contrast between the open moorlands and the cliff coast, with its succession of bustling seaside resorts, means that the trail is essentially two completely different experiences. Even at the outset some walkers questioned whether this trail should have been a circular walk, finishing back at Helmsley, but since that time the Tabular Hills Walk has been waymarked and is there to be walked if anyone chooses to complete a full circuit. The option also exists, of course, to finish the Cleveland Way at Filey Brigg and immediately embark upon the Yorkshire Wolds Way.

A gateway is passed on a moorland gap between Cold Moor and the Wainstones (Day 3)

Waymarks for the route are the standard national trail acorn logo, along with directional arrows. Signposts for the route may simply read Cleveland Way, or they may additionally give one of the next destinations along the trail. Keep up-to-date with developments and diversions by checking the website **www.nationaltrail.co.uk/clevelandway**, and obtain a current copy of the *Cleveland Way Accommodation and Information Guide* from National Park offices.

DAY 1
Helmsley to Sutton Bank

Start	Market cross, Helmsley, grid ref 613839
Finish	Visitor Centre, Sutton Bank, grid ref 515830
Distance	17km (10.5 miles)
Maps	OS Landranger 100, OS Explorer OL26
Terrain	Easy walking along clearly marked paths and tracks, from wooded dales to open fields and cliff edges.
Refreshments	Hambleton Hotel and Sutton Bank National Park Visitor Centre.
Public Transport	Helmsley is an important Moorsbus hub, with plenty of onward connections to points along the Cleveland Way, including Rievaulx, Sutton Bank, Carlton Bank and Clay Bank. Scarborough & District bus 128 links Helmsley with Sutton Bank and Scarborough.

The first day along the Cleveland Way sees the route leaving Helmsley and crossing over a wooded rise to Rievaulx, where a short detour takes in the substantial ruins of Rievaulx Abbey. The route climbs from wooded valleys to higher fields, reaching the steep western scarp slope at Sutton Bank. There is another short detour along the cliff edge of Roulston Scar to take in Kilburn White Horse, then the route doubles back on itself to allow an exploration of the National Park Visitor Centre at Sutton Bank. Lodgings are scarce around Sutton Bank, but there are good bus links back to Helmsley if required. Strong walkers who make an early start from Helmsley could press on towards Osmotherley for the night.

Leave the market cross at Market Place in **Helmsley** by following the road signposted for Stokesley, passing All Saints Church. Turn left along a road called Cleveland Way, signposted Footpath to Rievaulx. Note the Cleveland Way commemoration stone, just to the right of a car park, deeply carved with the names of some of the highlights of the route, many of which will become firm favourites

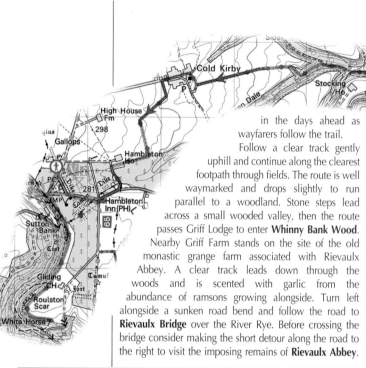

in the days ahead as wayfarers follow the trail.

Follow a clear track gently uphill and continue along the clearest footpath through fields. The route is well waymarked and drops slightly to run parallel to a woodland. Stone steps lead across a small wooded valley, then the route passes Griff Lodge to enter **Whinny Bank Wood**. Nearby Griff Farm stands on the site of the old monastic grange farm associated with Rievaulx Abbey. A clear track leads down through the woods and is scented with garlic from the abundance of ramsons growing alongside. Turn left alongside a sunken road bend and follow the road to **Rievaulx Bridge** over the River Rye. Before crossing the bridge consider making the short detour along the road to the right to visit the imposing remains of **Rievaulx Abbey**.

RIEVAULX ABBEY

Founded in 1132 by Walter l'Espec, Rievaulx Abbey was a Cistercian house. During its construction a short canal was built and rafts bore blocks of stone to the site. The abbey is built almost on a north–south axis rather than the usual east–west because of its situation in a rather narrow dale. Only 35 years after its foundation the abbey boasted 140 monks, 250 lay brothers and 260 hired laymen. Even in its ruinous state the walls rise to a prodigious height and give a good impression of the size and complexity of the building. There is an entrance charge for the abbey, and toilets outside the grounds.

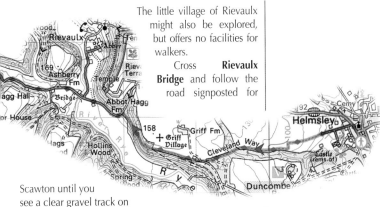

The little village of Rievaulx might also be explored, but offers no facilities for walkers.

Cross **Rievaulx Bridge** and follow the road signposted for Scawton until you see a clear gravel track on the right marked Cleveland Way. The track runs alongside a wood and passes a few shallow **fishing ponds** before the route crosses stepping-stones on the right. Walk to a nearby track and turn right to follow it up through a valley with forested sides. Keep left into **Flassen Dale** at a junction of tracks then watch for a more rugged track heading up a wooded valley on the right. This climbs out into large, gently sloping fields. Follow the clear track gradually uphill, then turn right as signposted along a path to reach the little village of **Cold Kirby** where the only facility is Mount Grace Farm bed-and-breakfast.

Limestone cliffs flank the North York Moors and drop steeply to the plains below

Rievaulx Abbey was founded in 1132 and remains a tall and imposing edifice

Follow the road up to the top end of the village, around 250m (820ft). Turn left as signposted, following a track through fields, then turn right, left and right again to walk alongside a forest. When a farm access road is reached near **Hambleton House** and its stables, turn left to follow it to the busy A170. Turn right and pass the **Hambleton Inn**, which offers food and drink. A little further along the road Cote Faw bed-and-breakfast offers the only convenient accommodation on the route.

A minor road on the left is signposted for the Yorkshire Gliding Club, while the Cleveland Way follows a path away from the road junction and through a patchy woodland to reach a clear path on a cliff edge at 290m (950ft). A three-fingered signpost at this point might cause confusion. The Cleveland Way officially turns left, but doubles back later to pass the same path junction. The apparent detour is well worth the effort, however, as it runs around the cliffs of **Roulston Scar** to reach the very head of the **Kilburn White Horse**, enjoying wide-ranging views across the plains. *Heed the warning signs around the airfield. Do not short cut across the airfield, watch out for low-flying gliders and do not tamper with towing cables.*

KILBURN WHITE HORSE

Only the head of the white horse can be seen from the Cleveland Way – you need to go down to a picnic site to see much more of the beast. It was cut in 1857 under the direction of local schoolmaster John Hodgson. The inspiration came from another local man, Thomas Taylor, who had witnessed the cleaning and maintenance of a white horse in the south. As the bedrock is oolitic limestone, rather than the white chalk found in the south, the Kilburn White Horse is given occasional applications of whitewash. The figure measures 96m (314ft) by 69m (228ft) and is a landmark for many on the lower plains. Of greater antiquity, cutting across the glider field, is the Casten Dike, which may have once formed a defensive or territorial boundary on the promontory.

The Cleveland Way runs near the National Park Visitor Centre on Sutton Bank

Double back along the cliff path and remain on the clearest path as signposted for **Sutton Bank** (author James Herriot had a special affection for the view from here). Either cross the busy A170 to pick up the Cleveland Way on the other side, just to the left, or make a detour to the right through a car park to reach the **National Park Visitor Centre**

NATIONAL PARK VISITOR CENTRE

The North York Moors National Park Visitor Centre catches tourists at one of the busiest entry points for the national park. Displays and exhibits focus on conservation in order to encourage sensitive and thoughtful recreation. Maps and guides are on sale and there is a restaurant and toilets on site. Frequent Scarborough & District bus 128 services run to and from Helmsley and Scarborough and there are connections with Moorsbus services. Accommodation is very limited in the area, but buses allow a speedy return to Helmsley if a wider range of options is needed.

DAY 2
Sutton Bank to Osmotherley

Start	Visitor Centre, Sutton Bank, grid ref 515830
Finish	Market cross, Osmotherley, grid ref 456973
Distance	18.5km (11.5 miles)
Maps	OS Landrangers 99 and 100, OS Explorer OL26
Terrain	Gentle cliff-top walking on good paths is followed by a clear track leading over high moorland. Field paths and tracks are used towards the end.
Refreshments	Sutton Bank National Park Visitor Centre. Pubs and cafés at Osmotherley.
Public Transport	Scarborough & District bus 128 links Sutton Bank with Helmsley and Scarborough. Moorsbus services offer onward links with Osmotherley, Carlton Bank and Clay Bank. Abbott's buses link Osmotherley with Northallerton and Stokesley.

This day's walk essentially traces the steep-sloping western edge of the North York Moors National Park. Although of modest altitude, never reaching as high as 400m (1300ft), views from the edge stretch far across the plains to the distant swellings of the Pennines. The Cleveland Way also begins to touch on the wilder fringes of the North York Moors, allowing walkers their first experience of the apparently endless expanses of heather moorland. The route includes part of the Hambleton Drove Road, an ancient upland thoroughfare with a long history. At the end of the day the little village of Osmotherley offers all a tired walker needs. Make the most of it, as there are some empty stretches ahead where facilities are sparse or absent.

Leave a bend at the top of the main A170 at **Sutton Bank** where the Cleveland Way is signposted for Sneck Yate. The path initially runs through patchy woodland at around 300m (985ft), with only occasional glimpses over the cliffs to the left. **Gormire Lake** is seen in a wooded hollow at the foot of the cliffs, with the plains stretching beyond.

Looking back along steep and wooded slopes to Gormire Lake and Sutton Bank

The cliff path is grassy and gently graded, dropping slightly as it turns right and later swings left. The cliffs become a wooded slope, then there is a gradual ascent onto **Boltby Scar** where grass and bilberry, along with contorted larches, cover the site of an Iron Age hill fort at 330m (1080ft). The nearby cliff is cleft by a 'windypit' chasm which afforded a crude habitation.

GORMIRE LAKE

This little lake is entirely natural, but unusual, since the area does not readily support lakes. It was formed when a huge section of the escarpment slumped onto the plains, the detached strata tilting back at an angle and leaving a small valley between itself and the freshly broken cliff face. The valley was filled with rubble and clay from the fracture, allowing water to pool in a hollow when normally it would have seeped through into the limestone bedrock. According to local lore the lake is bottomless – in reality it is quite shallow. The surrounding woodlands are home to red, fallow and roe deer, though these are seldom seen.

Descend gradually to pass above an old quarry and continue to **High Barn**, situated between two patches of woodland. Walk gently down to a gate, entering a wood and crossing a minor road on **Sneck Yate Bank**. Continue through more woodland and emerge onto another road, turning right to follow the road up a wooded slope and passing **High Paradise Farm**. Shortly after passing the farm turn left along **Hambleton Drove Road**, a broad, grassy enclosed track with fields to the left and moors to the right. Further along the old drove road a gate gives access to **Boltby Forest** and the track later leaves the forest at another gate at **Steeple Cross**.

Follow a long, grass-fringed track going gently uphill with heather moorland beyond. There is almost always a drystone wall over to the left and open moorland stretching away to the right. Views across the plains stretch to the distant Pennines. A tumbled ruin beside the track used to be **Limekiln House**, once a wayside inn frequented by drovers. Watch out for a left turn at **Whitestones** where the old drove road, still accompanied by the wall,

Map continues p.117

115

HAMBLETON DROVE ROAD

No doubt this ancient drove road was based on a prehistoric ridgeway route. Travellers and traders preferred to keep to the high ground rather than risk passage through the plains, which were once densely wooded, swampy in places, and inhabited by wild animals. Even long after the lowlands were tamed, drovers moving livestock from Scotland to London used the high ground to avoid enclosed farmland and expensive turnpikes. Covering immense distances, they could get a good price when stock was scarce around the capital. The 18th and 19th centuries saw brisk trade, with herds of up to a thousand animals on the move. As drovers could be charged 1s/6d (7.5 pence) per score of cattle to use a turnpike, great savings were made by avoiding them altogether.

Steeple Cross may not have been a true wayside cross, but a stone marker for routes that branched from the old drove road.

Walkers follow the course of the Hambleton
Drove Road towards a forested area

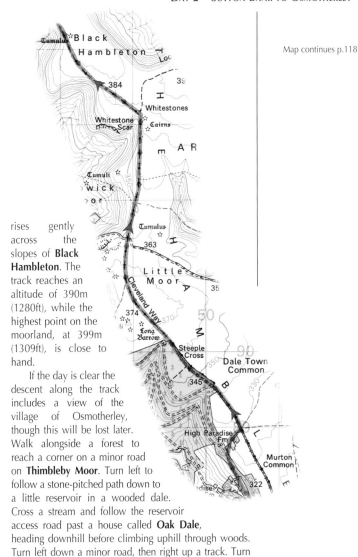

Map continues p.118

rises gently across the slopes of **Black Hambleton**. The track reaches an altitude of 390m (1280ft), while the highest point on the moorland, at 399m (1309ft), is close to hand.

If the day is clear the descent along the track includes a view of the village of Osmotherley, though this will be lost later. Walk alongside a forest to reach a corner on a minor road on **Thimbleby Moor**. Turn left to follow a stone-pitched path down to a little reservoir in a wooded dale. Cross a stream and follow the reservoir access road past a house called **Oak Dale**, heading downhill before climbing uphill through woods. Turn left down a minor road, then right up a track. Turn

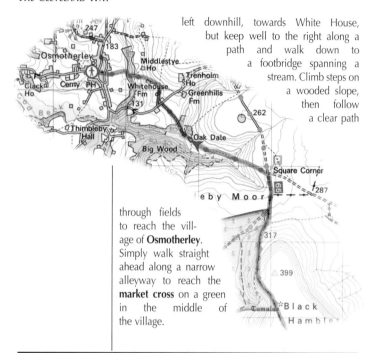

left downhill, towards White House, but keep well to the right along a path and walk down to a footbridge spanning a stream. Climb steps on a wooded slope, then follow a clear path through fields to reach the village of **Osmotherley**. Simply walk straight ahead along a narrow alleyway to reach the **market cross** on a green in the middle of the village.

OSMOTHERLEY

Osmotherley is a charming stone village with a green heart. Three roads meet at the market cross and nearby is a stone table on five legs where baskets of market produce were sold. John Wesley preached from this stone table, and the Methodist chapel in the village has a date-stone of 1754.

Facilities in the village include a handful of accommodation options, from a hotel to bed-and-breakfasts. The youth hostel and campsite are just outside the village – walk up North End to reach them. There is a post office, a pub and a few shops, including the Walking Shop if you need any outdoor gear. Moorsbus services run from Osmotherley to Carlton Bank on the Cleveland Way, as well as to Guisborough. Abbott's buses run through the village, offering links with Northallerton and Stokesley. Be sure to visit the award-winning toilets in the village!

DAY 3
Osmotherley to Clay Bank

Start	Market cross, Osmotherley, grid ref 456973
Finish	B1257, Clay Bank, grid ref 573033
Distance	18km (11 miles)
Maps	OS Landrangers 93 and 99, OS Explorer OL26
Terrain	A series of forest walks, hill climbs and exposed high moor lands. Some paths are quite steep and rugged.
Refreshments	Pub off-route at Swainby. Café at Carlton Bank. Possibly a snack van at Clay Bank.
Public Transport	Moorsbus services link Osmotherley with Carlton Bank, Clay Bank and Guisborough. Abbott's buses link Osmotherley with Northallerton and Stokesley. Take note of Moorsbus services at Clay Bank if you want to use the bus to reach Great Broughton or Chop Gate.

This part of the Cleveland Way is remarkably hilly, rather like a monstrous roller coaster. On a clear day, with time to enjoy the surroundings, it is also a very scenic and enjoyable stretch, but in foul weather there is little shelter from the elements and the sight of yet another steep climb can be dispiriting. While strong walkers could combine this with the next day's walk to Kildale, the total distance and the effort involved would be daunting for some. Breaking the journey at Clay Bank means that you have to follow the road one way or the other, to Great Broughton or Chop Gate, in search of accommodation. With careful reference to the Moorsbus timetable, however, you can avoid the road walk by arriving at Clay Bank in time to catch a bus. Bear in mind that you need to plan ahead and ensure you are back on the bus at the right time in the morning to continue walking from Clay Bank to Kildale.

Leave **Osmotherley** by following the road called North End and turn left at the top of the village as signposted for the Cleveland Way. Follow a stony access road past a

LADY CHAPEL

This old chapel, attached to a house, is said to have been built by Catherine of Aragon, first wife of Henry VIII, in 1515 for the recluse Thomas Parkinson. A number of miracles are said to have taken place there and the chapel remains a popular site of pilgrimage, being reached by a track lined with the Stations of the Cross.

few houses, continuing uphill to a fork. Lady Chapel is signposted up to the right and worth a short detour, but the Cleveland Way is signposted to the left, running close to **Chapel Wood Farm**.

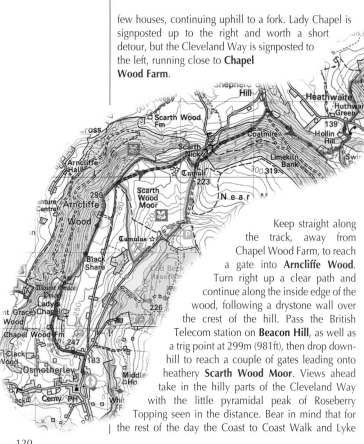

Keep straight along the track, away from Chapel Wood Farm, to reach a gate into **Arncliffe Wood**. Turn right up a clear path and continue along the inside edge of the wood, following a drystone wall over the crest of the hill. Pass the British Telecom station on **Beacon Hill**, as well as a trig point at 299m (981ft), then drop downhill to reach a couple of gates leading onto heathery **Scarth Wood Moor**. Views ahead take in the hilly parts of the Cleveland Way with the little pyramidal peak of Roseberry Topping seen in the distance. Bear in mind that for the rest of the day the Coast to Coast Walk and Lyke

Wake Walk run essentially along the same course as the Cleveland Way. A clear, paved path runs down the moorland slope, then a left turn leads down a

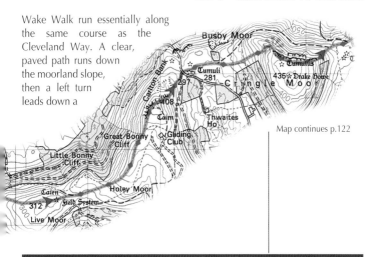

Map continues p.122

MOUNT GRACE PRIORY

Off-route, but worthy of note, is Mount Grace Priory, reached by detouring downhill through Arncliffe Wood. This was a Carthusian monastery founded in 1398 by Thomas de Holand. Of particular interest are the two-storey monk's cells around the cloister, one of which has been restored to its original condition. Each cell had a living room, study, bedroom and small herb garden. The central tower of the priory church remains intact. (There is an entrance charge.)

SCARTH NICK

A stagnant mass of ice melting on higher ground caused a torrent of glacial melt-water to pour through a gap in the hills, cutting Scarth Nick. The road at Scarth Nick is steep but otherwise innocuous. However, in the 18th century the well-travelled Arthur Young was scathing about it, saying, 'The going down into Cleveland is beyond all description terrible…for you go through such steep, rough, narrow, rocky precipices that I would sincerely advise any friend to go a hundred miles to avoid it.'

steeper pitched path to reach a minor road at **Scarth Nick**.

Cross a cattle-grid to find a signpost pointing along a clear woodland path at **Coalmire**.

Continue straight along a woodland track then later head down to the left. A stone at this point commemorates Bill Cowley, a local farmer who founded the classic Lyke Wake Walk across the moors from Osmotherley to

Looking back along the Cleveland Way from the top of the climb onto Live Moor

Ravenscar. There is access through a gate at the bottom end of the wood to the nearby village of **Swainby** (post office, shop, pub and guesthouse), but turn right without going through the gate to stay inside the wood, enjoying the sight of huge oak trees. Watch for a left turn later which leads out of the wood and down through a field, linking with a track crossing two rivers in the wooded valley of **Scugdale**. Walk up a farm road to reach a road junction beside a telephone at **Huthwaite Green**.

The Cleveland Way is signposted to the right of the telephone box, up a woodland path, passing ironstone spoil heaps where there are open views across the valley and plains. There is a sudden right turn up a steep, stone-pitched path on a wooded slope, then continue climbing less steeply up a stone-paved moorland path. This levels out as it crosses the 312m (1024ft) summit of **Live Moor**, where views are wide-ranging around the North York Moors.

Cross a broad and heathery dip in the moorland then climb again on **Holey Moor**, passing alongside a **gliding club** field. A trig point is reached at 408m (1338ft) alongside a stone upright on **Carlton Moor**. Enjoy splendid views across the plains, from the distant Pennines to industrial Teesdale, past the little peak of Roseberry Topping, around the North York Moors and back along the Cleveland Way in the direction of Osmotherley. Follow the stone-paved path steeply down to a gap, passing close to a quarried edge protected by a fence. Cross a track and a road on the lower slopes of Carlton Bank (the road has a Moorsbus service linking with Osmotherley and Guisborough). Continue onwards, but note the immediate access to **Lord Stones Café** and toilets in a car park surrounded by trees. The café is not too apparent as it is largely buried underground! Camping is available too.

Walk across a grassy common to leave the café, then follow a grassy track flanked by a fence and drystone wall, go through a gate and continue up a paved path close to the wall. A stone viewpoint seat dedicated to local rambler Alec Falconer is reached at

The view back along the way from
Cringle End to Lord Stones and Carlton Bank

Cringle End. Climb higher along a gritty path and a paved path along the top of the abrupt northern edge of **Cringle Moor**, around 420m (1380ft). A steep, winding, stone-pitched path leads downhill, passing shale spoil before reaching a fork at a gap. Keep right at the fork to go through a gate, then follow another steep, stone-pitched path over the top of **Cold Moor** at 401m (1316ft). Drop down to another gate and another grassy gap.

The next steep climb passes to the left of jagged, blocky **Wain Stones**, which are worth studying from all angles and completely out of character with the smooth contours prevalent around the North York Moors. Once above them a delightful level path runs along a moorland edge at 390m (1280ft) on **Hasty Bank**. At the end of this lofty promenade there is a steep path downhill, later following a wall down to the B1257 at **Clay Bank**.

The jagged, blocky Wainstones are popular with rock-climbers and photographers

Alternative Route

Those contemplating this walk on a day of foul weather should bear in mind that there are paths and tracks cutting across the northern slopes of the hills between Carlton Bank and Clay Bank. The first part of this low-level route is known as the Miners' Track and is then followed by forest tracks. The miners worked these slopes for alum, jet and ironstone.

Reaching the road on **Clay Bank** is not strictly the end of the day's walk. Strong walkers may well cross the road and continue to Kildale, while others who have studied the Moorsbus timetable will catch a bus down to **Great Broughton** or **Chop Gate**, the two nearest villages, located in opposite directions and offering accommodation, food and drink. The alternative is to walk to these places, both of which are 4km (2.5 miles) off-route, a distance that might have to be repeated the following morning if there is no bus. A snack van might be available at a nearby forest car park on the Great Broughton side of the gap, but don't rely on it being there.

CHOP GATE

This hamlet is located down the road in Bilsdale and facilities are limited to the Buck Inn, offering food, drink and accommodation (there are toilets too). Moorsbus services link with Guisborough and Osmotherley.

GREAT BROUGHTON

This village is located on the plains. There is a hotel offering food, drink and accommodation, and an inn offering food, drink and a campsite. There is also a post office shop, while Moorsbus services link with Guisborough and Osmotherley.

DAY 4
Clay Bank to Kildale

Start	B1257, Clay Bank, grid ref 573033
Finish	Kildale post office, grid ref 606094
Distance	15km (9.5 miles)
Maps	OS Landrangers 93 and 94, OS Explorer OL26
Terrain	High and exposed moorlands, but good paths and tracks. Care is needed with route-finding in poor visibility.
Refreshment	None along the route, then limited to a couple of tea gardens at Kildale.
Public Transport	Moorsbus offers limited services to Clay Bank from the nearby villages of Great Broughton and Chop Gate. Kildale is served by daily Arriva trains from Middlesbrough and Whitby.

This is the most remote part of the Cleveland Way, traversing the highest part of the North York Moors and with no easy access to facilities of any kind. Accommodation, food and drink are limited even at Kildale at the end of the day. Walkers who cannot secure lodgings in Kildale and do not wish to cover any more of the route during the day should remember to check the times of trains passing through the village. These offer links with nearby villages and even distant towns such as Whitby and Middlesbrough. In foul weather walkers need to keep a careful eye on their maps – paths and tracks are generally clear, but a wrong turning at a junction could involve a huge detour. In calm, clear weather this is one of the most memorable parts of the route, especially when the heather moorlands are flushed purple in the summer.

Leave the B1257 at **Clay Bank** and follow a steep, stone-pitched path uphill alongside a wall. Go through a gate at the top of the slope and the path runs at an easier gradient across the higher moorlands. The broad crest is called **Carr Ridge** and rises to around 380m (1250ft). There are fine views back to the hilly parts of the

Looking back towards Clay Bank while climbing onto the broad Urra Moor

Cleveland Way, but now the terrain, although remote and exposed, is gentler. The path is mostly gritty, with grass, heather or bilberry alongside, although a few short stretches are paved with stone. Keep left, roughly along the crest of **Urra Moor**, until passing close to a trig point. This actually sits on a burial mound on **Round Hill** at 454m (1490ft). It can be reached by a short diversion along a path and is the highest point on the moors, as well as in the whole of this guidebook! Note the Hand Stone and Face Stone beside the track, which are old route markers on the moor.

ROUND HILL

The trig point on Round Hill sits on the squat remains of a moorland burial mound. The North York Moors are dotted with similar mounds, and some parts are crisscrossed by ancient earthworks that were either territorial markers or defensive structures. The moorland marker stones are of more recent antiquity, dating from around the 18th century. The Hand Stone has two open palms, on them the words, 'This way to Stoxla' (Stokesley) and 'This way to Kirbie' (Kirkbymoorside). The older Face Stone features a crude face.

Continue along the clearest track, then keep left at a fork. Later watch out for a path, marked only by a cairn on the left, which offers a short cut away from the main route.

Map continues p.131

Short cut

The short cut runs down to an old railway trackbed. Turn left to follow the track to the top of an incline, then keep right to climb uphill a short way to link with another high track and turn left to continue along the main route.

The main route stays on the clear track then cuts across a moorland hollow, as marked, to reach an old railway trackbed. Turn right as signposted Cleveland Way and walk towards a gate. Beyond the gate turn left at an intersection of tracks at **Bloworth Crossing**, also signposted Cleveland Way. The Coast to Coast Walk, incidentally, runs straight ahead at Bloworth Crossing and is not seen again until close to Robin Hood's Bay.

129

THE ROSEDALE RAILWAY

The Rosedale Mineral Railway operated from 1861 to 1929, during which time it transported iron ore from Rosedale to the blast furnaces of Durham. The line contoured along the upper slopes of Rosedale and Farndale, as high as 410m (1345ft), before reaching a sudden 1:5 incline on Greenhow Bank. Cottages at the top of the incline were known as Siberia by the workers, owing to their remoteness. Loaded wagons had to be lowered three at a time from a winding house, while empty wagons were drawn back up the line. The remote Bloworth Crossing was manned by a keeper at a time when the old road over the moor carried more traffic than it does today. The keeper lived beside the level crossing in a lonely house which has long been demolished.

Jenny Bradley's Cross stands beside a taller stone pillar near Bloworth Crossing

Follow the stony track gently uphill, passing a pair of upright stones. The taller stone is relatively modern, dated 1888, while the shorter one is considerably older and known as **Jenny Bradley's Cross**. The high moorland track seems to run on forever when seen from **Greenhow Bank**. Look out for the **guide stone** away to the right.

STONE CROSSES

Jenny Bradley sounds like the name of a person, but 'Bradley' is thought to derive from 'Broad Ley', or a broad trackway. Jenny Bradley's Cross is a little stump of a stone cross that merely marks an old track over the moors, and the taller stone is a 19th-century boundary stone between moorland estates.

The 18th-century guide stone is easily missed in poor visibility, lying further away from the track. It offers the following directions: 'Ingleby and Stoxley' (Stokesley), 'Kirby (Kirkbymoorside) and Helmsley', and 'Gisbro' (Guisborough). Of interest to cash-strapped walkers is a hollow on top of the stone that usually contains a few coins. From 1711 it was a requirement that signposts and guidestones were erected on routes such as this, though the stone markers outlived the wooden ones.

Keep walking northwards along the track, across **Ingleby Moor**, until another track signposted for the Cleveland Way branches off to the right at a gate. This track leads along another moorland crest over **Battersby Moor**, eventually reaching a gate at a road bend. Follow the road straight ahead, but note that a right turn down the road leads to remote Shepherd's House farmhouse bed-and-breakfast. The road crosses a rise on **Kildale Moor**, turns left at a corner, then runs down around the slopes of **Park Nab** to reach a broad and green valley. When a road junction is reached, turn right for **Kildale**.

Horse-riders enjoy following the high track across Battersby Moor above Kildale

KILDALE

This small village has only limited facilities, including a post office shop with tea garden, another tea garden at Glebe Cottage, nearby Bankside House bed-and-breakfast and a camping barn at Low Farm. If accommodation cannot be secured here or within walking distance, then go down to the railway station where daily Arriva trains allow other nearby villages, or more distant Whitby and Middlesbrough, to be reached. There are toilets at the railway station.

A quiet road passes Park Nab on the final descent from the moors to Kildale

DAY 5
Kildale to Saltburn-by-the-Sea

Start	Kildale post office, grid ref 606094
Finish	Saltburn-by-the-Sea, grid ref 666215
Distance	24km (15 miles)
Maps	OS Landrangers 93 and 94, OS Explorer OL26
Terrain	Forest and moorland tracks are generally clear, but care is needed at junctions. Easy field paths give way to suburban walking on pavements.
Refreshments	Pub at Slapewath, more pubs at Skelton Green and Skelton. Plenty of pubs, cafés and restaurants at Saltburn.
Public Transport	Arriva rail services link Kildale with Whitby and Middlesbrough. Arriva bus 93 passes Slapewath, near Guisborough, linking with Middlesbrough, Whitby, Robin Hood's Bay and Scarborough. Frequent Arriva buses serve Skelton and Saltburn-by-the-Sea, while Saltburn also has regular Arriva bus and train services to and from Middlesbrough.

The route now enters Captain Cook Country, visiting Captain Cook's Monument on Easby Moor. An abiding feature along the Cleveland Way so far has been the occasional view of Roseberry Topping. Walkers now come face to face with it, and while many choose to climb it, others pass it by. An ascent is part of the *official* route, but it does represent extra effort and a retracing of steps. The bustling town of Guisborough can be seen, but the route passes high above it through Guisborough Forest. The North York Moors National Park is left behind for a while at Slapewath, and the route wanders through Skelton to reach Saltburn-by-the-Sea. After those remote moorland days with sparse facilities for walkers, the Cleveland Way now reaches the cliff coastline where accommodation options abound and food and drink are plentiful.

Starting from the post office in **Kildale**, turn left as sign-posted for Kildale railway station, but turn right at Glebe

Captain Cook's Monument, erected on Easby Moor, is a prominent landmark

Cottage Tea Garden. Follow the road under the railway, cross the River Leven and climb past **Bankside Farm**, which offers bed-and-breakfast. Turn left at the top of the road to follow a forest track along the crest of **Coate Moor**. Branch left along a gravel forest path signposted the Cleveland Way. Walk straight through the woods then climb up a paved path that leads onto heathery **Easby Moor**. Head straight for the prominent stone obelisk which is **Captain Cook's Monument**, standing at 324m (1063ft).

CAPTAIN COOK'S MONUMENT

This fine stone obelisk stands 15m (51ft) high and overlooks Marton, the sub-urb of Middlesbrough where James Cook was born in 1728, and Great Ayton, where he received an education from 1736 to 1740. Cook's father was employed at Airy Holme Farm, where Mr Scottowe paid for James' education at the Michael Postgate School, now the Captain Cook Schoolroom Museum. The inscription on the obelisk reads, 'In memory of Captain Cook the cele-brated navigator. A man in nautical knowledge inferior to none. In zeal, prudence and energy superior to most. Regardless of the danger he opened an intercourse with the Friendly Isles and other parts of the Southern Hemisphere. Born at Marton in 1728. Massacred at Owhyee (Hawaii) 1779.'

Follow a stone-paved path away from the monument and walk down a path and track on a forested slope. Turn right along a minor road, then almost immediately left up a flight of steps. The gradient eases on **Great Ayton Moor**, where there is a wall and forest to the left and open heather moorland to the right. Simply follow a clear track onwards, around 290m (950ft), with the wall always to the left. The wall suddenly turns a corner on **Newton Moor** where there is a gate and a signpost for **Roseberry Topping**.

ROSEBERRY TOPPING

Quarried and scarred, undermined for ironstone, leading to partial collapse in 1907, Roseberry Topping has suffered greatly through the years but has by no means been diminished. The 'Yorkshire Matterhorn' bears its scars proudly and presents an aggressive face to the plains. The detour to the summit is an *official* part of the Cleveland Way, but some walkers take one look and decide they can do without the exercise on its admittedly steep slopes. Climb it or don't climb it – the choice is yours. Omitting it will save 2km (1.25 miles) from the day's walk, but it may always irk you later that you never did climb it!

Go through the gate if you wish to climb Roseberry Topping. The path is paved as it drops steeply downhill, then levels out on a grassy gap. Another stone-paved

135

path winds steeply up the rugged slopes of **Roseberry Topping** to reach bare sandstone slabs and a trig point at 320m (1050ft). Enjoy the views from this airy perch, looking out across the plains to the distant Pennines and industrial Teesmouth, as well as to the North York Moors closer by. Retrace your steps back across the gap to return to the gate in the corner of the wall on **Newton Moor**.

Map continues p.138

Head along a clear, gritty path that cuts straight across the heather moorland. Turn right after a small gate to walk between a fence and a forest. Turn right at another gate to leave the

GUISBOROUGH

forest and follow a rather battered track up a moorland slope for a short way. Watch for a path heading off to the left, running down into a dip in the moorland, then walk uphill alongside a wall with **Highcliffe Farm** only a couple of fields away to the left. Turn left as signposted Cleveland Way at a corner of **Guisborough Forest**.

Walk down a path in the forest and turn right, climbing across a track at a metal Tees Link signpost. This route links the Cleveland Way and Teesdale Way, but don't follow it. A stone-pitched path climbs up alongside an old quarry on **Highcliff Nab**, then a left turn runs along the top edge of the quarry where there is a fine view over the busy little town of **Guisborough**. Follow a track onwards through the forest then fork down to the left at a junction of tracks. Keep walking straight ahead, but watch for a sudden turn uphill to the right. Though steep, the route soon levels out and walkers simply keep straight ahead again, more or less on a level. Head straight through an intersection of tracks and later there is a turn down to the left, running alongside the forest.

View of Roseberry Topping's distinctive outline on the descent from Easby Moor

GUISBOROUGH

Although off-route Guisborough does attract the attention of walkers, and can be reached easily enough either by making a detour on foot or by catching a bus from Slapewath. The cobbled High Street is full of character, but the town's centrepiece is Gisborough Priory. This was an Augustinian house, founded in 1119 by Robert de Brus, but rebuilt after being destroyed by a fire in 1289 (there is an entrance charge). Also of interest are the Guisborough Museum and the nearby Guisborough Forest and Walkway Visitor Centre.

Facilities in Guisborough include accommodation, banks with ATMs, a post office, toilets, plenty of pubs, internationally flavoured restaurants and shops. There is a tourist information centre beside Gisborough Priory, tel 01287 633801. Regular Arriva bus services run from Guisborough to Middlesbrough, and Arriva bus 93 runs ahead to Whitby, Robin Hood's Bay and Scarborough. This bus service can also be caught at Slapewath on the Cleveland Way.

Watch for a stile on the right to follow a path out of the forest, then turn left down a concrete road on a wooded slope. Turn right at a **cattle-grid** to walk along the lower edge of the wood. Keep off a broad, bare terrace of crushed alum-shale spoil and instead follow a path beside a woodland fence as marked and signposted Cleveland Way. Keep an eye on directional arrow markers, basically contouring across a wooded slope before turning left down to the busy main A171. Turn left along the main road, then right to reach **Slapewath** where the Fox and Hounds offers food, drink and accommodation.

Walk away from the Fox and Hounds to nearby cottages where a path rises to an **old quarry**. Keep to the right-hand side of the quarry, climbing steps up a slope of gorse bushes. When the upper edge of the quarry is reached, climb straight uphill then turn right uphill beside a field. A track leads past **Airy Hill Farm** to reach the little village of **Skelton Green**. Walk along Airy Hill Lane to reach a road junction near the **Green Inn**.

Cross the road and follow a tarmac path onwards

through fields. This enjoys a view towards Skelton Castle before dropping down to a narrow road. Turn right along the road then left down a flight of steps into **Skelton**. Cross the busy A173 and continue straight ahead. Turn right at the first road junction and follow this suburban road as it bends left downhill. Turn right into a field at the bottom as sign-posted. Veer left on entering the field, then turn left to walk straight past a housing development. Cross a road and walk straight onwards, then turn right in a wooded patch and go beneath the A174 bypass.

A clear woodland path leads downhill, turning a sharp bend to reach **Skelton Beck**. Cross a footbridge and go through a towering arch, one of 11 supporting

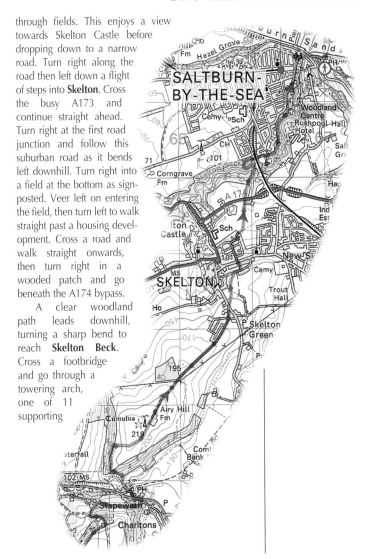

SKELTON GREEN AND SKELTON

Skelton Green is a small village with three pubs available for thirsty walkers, as well as Arriva and Boroughbus services to and from Saltburn and Middlesbrough. Skelton is a larger and busier village with the same bus connections, as well as a post office, more pubs and a variety of shops.

a monumental brick viaduct in use since 1872. When an **ornamental seat** is reached turn right, but keep high on the wooded slope. Later, turn right downhill, catching the garlic scent of ramsons in the woods, then fork left uphhill, as marked, into **Saltburn-by-the-Sea**. Turn right along the road and either keep right until it leads down to the sandy beach, or take one of the roads on the left into the town centre for a full range of services.

SALTBURN-BY-THE-SEA

Saltburn was originally no more than a huddle of cottages at the foot of the cliffs. Its smuggling history is remembered at Saltburn Smugglers Heritage Centre, set in some old fishermen's cottages where displays follow the story of John Andrew, known as 'the king of the smugglers'. The opening of a railway in 1861 transformed the place, and the elegant new town built on top of the cliffs was a quintessential Victorian spa resort. In 1869 a pier stretching 450m (1500ft) out to sea was constructed, but it has been damaged on a number of occasions by storm and shipwreck and is rather shorter these days. A hydraulic cliff lift was built in 1884 to spare people trudging endlessly up and down the steep slope between the town and the beach. Like many old seaside resorts Saltburn's grandeur has faded, but it remains an interesting place and walkers will find it offers much after the lonely moors.

Facilities in Saltburn include a good range of accommodation, banks with ATMs, a post office, toilets, plenty of pubs, restaurants and tearooms, as well as a splendid range of shops. The tourist information centre is by the railway station, tel 01287 622422. Arriva bus 62 (or 762 on Sundays and bank holidays) runs through town, offering regular links with Middlesbrough and Skinningrove. Express service X4 runs from Saltburn to Middlesbrough via Redcar, but not on Sundays. Arriva trains run daily to and from Middlesbrough and Darlington.

A view from the pier of the cliff lift and seaside resort of Saltburn-by-the-Sea

DAY 6
Saltburn-by-the-Sea to Sandsend

Start	Saltburn-by-the-Sea, grid ref 666215
Finish	Sandsend, grid ref 863125
Distance	27km (17 miles)
Maps	OS Landranger 94, OS Explorers OL26 and OL27
Terrain	Cliff coastal walking involving some steep ascents and descents. Parts of the route use field paths set back from the cliff. Village streets require careful route-finding. High tides at Runswick Bay may cover the beach walk.
Refreshments	Pub and café at Skinningrove. Staithes has several pubs and cafés. Pub off-route at Port Mulgrave. Runswick Bay has pubs and a beach café. Sandsend has pubs and restaurants.
Public Transport	Arriva bus 62 (or 762 on Sunday and bank holidays) links Saltburn with Middlesbrough and Skinningrove. Bus X56 links Staithes, Runswick Bay and Sandsend with Middlesbrough and Whitby.

The Cleveland Way enjoys its first day along the coast, taking in splendid cliffs and coves. After leaving Saltburn the route traverses Hunt Cliff to reach industrial Skinningrove, then climbs over Boulby Cliff, the highest cliff on the east coast of England, to descend to the charming and colourful harbour village of Staithes. This is where the young James Cook worked as a shopkeeper's assistant and was inspired by the comings and goings of seafarers to consider a change of career. The Captain Cook and Staithes Heritage Centre offers plenty of background information. The cliff coast continues to Runswick Bay, a lovely little village on a steep slope facing a blue bay fringed by golden sands. This might be far enough for some walkers, but it is worth continuing to Sandsend to finish just short of Whitby, so that this old whaling town can be explored early the next morning.

Leave **Saltburn-by-the-Sea** by walking down the road past the Spa Hotel to reach the beach. Alternatively, if there is time to spare, use any of the paths on the steep grassy slopes between the town and the beach. Turn right to walk to the **Ship Inn**, a former haunt of smugglers, passing boats and rusty tractors on the sand and shingle beach on the way. Climb steps behind the inn to reach a grassy cliff top, passing a marker stone for the Cleveland Heritage Coast and later passing a sign for the Hunt Cliff Nature Reserve. **Hunt Cliff** has plenty of ledges where fulmars and kittiwakes nest, while cormorants are also commonly observed. The grasslands along the cliff tops are one of the few places in the country where 'dyer's-greenweed' grows. The flowers of this small shrub yield a yellow dye which used to be mixed with woad to create the colour 'Kendal green'.

HUNT CLIFF ROMAN SIGNAL STATION

Until recently the site of a Roman signal station was passed on Hunt Cliff, but it has since been lost over the cliff edge. It was probably constructed around 367AD, and may have been attacked and the last of its occupants slain, as 14 bodies were found dumped in an adjacent well when the site was excavated. The station was linked by line of sight with other stations along the coast at Goldsborough, Ravenscar, Scarborough, Filey Brigg and Flamborough Head, each one intended to keep a lookout for sea-borne invaders.

At over 100m (330ft) above sea level the path finds itself hemmed in between the cliffs and a railway line which serves a steelworks at Skinningrove and the Boulby Potash Mine. A couple of intriguing **ironwork sculptures** stand beside the path and there are good views both ways along the cliff coast. Walk gradually downhill, then go down steps on the left to continue along a strip of sand dunes spiked with marram grass. The 'cliff' above is actually formed from slag from the steelworks, dumped in a molten state and then rapidly solidifying. Go through a gap in a concrete jetty and walk round the tiny harbour at **Skinningrove**, crossing a bridge to reach a small boatyard with tractors.

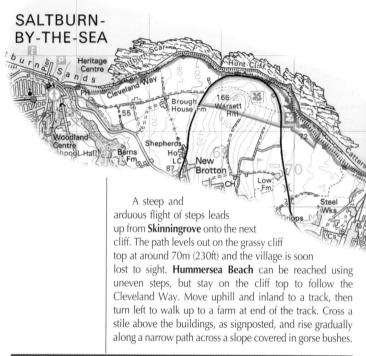

SALTBURN-
BY-THE-SEA

A steep and arduous flight of steps leads up from **Skinningrove** onto the next cliff. The path levels out on the grassy cliff top at around 70m (230ft) and the village is soon lost to sight. **Hummersea Beach** can be reached using uneven steps, but stay on the cliff top to follow the Cleveland Way. Move uphill and inland to a track, then turn left to walk up to a farm at end of the track. Cross a stile above the buildings, as signposted, and rise gradually along a narrow path across a slope covered in gorse bushes.

SKINNINGROVE

This industrial village looks a little down-at-heel, with some houses standing empty, while allotment huts and pigeon lofts look rather huddled and forlorn. It was no more than a quiet fishing cove until 1850, but it was transformed once the local ironstone began to be worked and a thriving steelworks was built – then it became known as 'the valley of iron'. The steelworks survives as a shadow of itself, yet occupies a site as big as the village. A short detour inland, signposted for the Riverside Building, reveals a pub, café, shop, toilets and a Mining Museum. Arriva bus 62 (or 762 on Sundays and bank holidays) offers regular links with Saltburn and Middlesbrough.

Cross a stile and continue up across a rugged slope, bearing right at a fork. The path along the top of **Boulby Cliff** overlooks the extensive **Loftus Alum Quarries** (you can read about the alum industry on an information board). Take care near the cliff edge, and beware the deep fissures along the clifftop too. Enjoy extensive views ahead along the coastal path and back along the course of the Cleveland Way towards Guisborough Forest, with the North York Moors beyond. The North York Moors National Park is entered again as the route climbs onto the highest part of the cliffs, at 203m (666ft) above sea level.

Map continues p.150

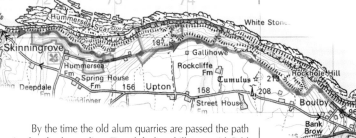

By the time the old alum quarries are passed the path is already descending. Turn left downhill to avoid fields ahead, then turn right along the lower cliffs to pass a row of former alum workers' cottages at **Boulby**. Walk down a

Walkers climb steeply from Skinningrove, with Hunt Cliff seen in the far distance

View along the coast from Boulby Cliff, the highest cliff on England's east coast

narrow road to **Boulby Lodge** then continue straight along a grassy path through the fields. The **Boulby Potash Mine** can be seen inland.

BOULBY POTASH MINE

This is the only potash mine in the country. It has been operating since 1973 and at the time of writing produces 16,000 tonnes per day, but the mineral is not easily won. The shafts here drop to a depth of 1500m (4900ft) at up to 7km (4.5 miles) out beneath the North Sea, deeper than any other mine in the country. The beds being mined were deposited from an extremely saline, landlocked sea in the Permian period, around 230 million years ago. Most of the mining is done by remote control, temperatures being above 40°C even before the machines start cutting, and despite cooling from a powerful ventilation system. The roof of the mine has to be preserved at all costs, since a breach would allow overlying soft marl to 'flow' into the mine under pressure. Potash has many uses in the chemical industry, but is chiefly used for agricultural fertiliser.

The path from **Boulby Lodge** reaches a crumbling cliff edge, so walk along the road, which has itself been moved inland on occasions. It is restricted to local traffic and leads down to the charming, colourful village of **Staithes.** Cross the footbridge over the narrow harbour to reach the main part of the village.

STAITHES

The narrow, natural harbour, with its protective projecting cliff face at Cowbar Nab, made Staithes an ideal retreat for fishermen, traders and smugglers. Latterly the higgledy-piggledy houses and narrow alleys have enchanted artists and photographers. For a thorough grounding in the history of this delightfully jumbled village, be sure to visit the Captain Cook and Staithes Heritage Centre. The teenage James Cook worked as an assistant to a shopkeeper called William Sanderson in Staithes. The sea destroyed the original shop, but parts of it were incorporated into Captain Cook's Cottage. Cook stayed only for 18 months, then moved to Whitby to train as an apprentice seaman and embark on his seafaring career.

Facilities in Staithes include a little accommodation, post office, toilets, a few pubs, cafés and shops. Arriva bus X56 runs from Staithes Lane End ahead to Runswick Bay, Sandsend and Whitby, or back to Skelton, Guisborough and Middlesbrough.

The charming, huddled village of Staithes sits in a narrow, natural tidal inlet

PORT MULGRAVE

Although the broken remains of a small harbour can be seen at Port Mulgrave, access from the tiny village seems restricted. In fact access to the harbour was through underground tunnels originating far inland at the Grinkle ironstone mines, so there was no need for any road link from the village. Ironstone was later removed from Grinkle by rail, and as the tunnels were no longer needed they were closed, leaving the harbour unused by 1916.

After crossing the footbridge over the harbour at **Staithes,** walk up to a narrow, cobbled street and turn left. The pub called the **Cod and Lobster** is reached, which has been partially demolished by storms three times. Turn right up Church Street and pass **Captain Cook's Cottage.** Follow the stone-paved Cleveland Way even further uphill to leave the village, taking a last fond look back at the intriguing jumble of cottages.

Turn left, as signposted for Runswick Bay, and follow a clear path past a farm. Walk through fields and climb a steep grassy slope to regain the cliff path. Keep climbing uphill, almost to 100m (330ft) on **Beacon Hill.** The next road, Rosedale Lane, could be followed inland from **Port Mulgrave** to reach the Ship Inn for food and drink, otherwise stay on the route.

The Cleveland Way is signposted off a corner of the road and along the top of the rugged slope known as **Rosedale Cliffs.** Follow the path around **Lingrow Cliffs** to reach a small pond, then turn right inland to reach the Runswick Bay Hotel at **Runswick Bank Top.** Turn left along the road to pass the Cliffemount Hotel and walk down a narrow road closed to vehicles. Continue down to the beach at **Runswick Bay.**

RUNSWICK BAY

This delightful little village is stacked up a steep slope facing a curved bay with a fine sandy beach. Despite its obvious beauty the situation looks precarious. One night in 1664, when most of the villagers were attending a funeral wake, the houses started to slip into the sea. By morning every dwelling was in ruins, except, for some mysterious reason, the house of the dead man. Some claim that this house is the one now known as Jubilee Cottage. A sea wall protects the current village from landslip. A thatched cottage was formerly inhabited by the coastguard, who would have had one of the best vantage points to observe all the comings and goings around the bay.

Facilities around Runswick Bay include a few hotels, bed-and-breakfasts and a campsite, toilets, pubs and a beach café. Arriva bus X56 runs regularly from the Runswick Bay Hotel ahead to Sandsend and Whitby, or back to Staithes, Skelton, Guisborough and Middlesbrough.

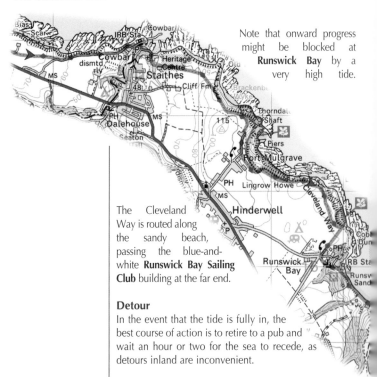

Note that onward progress might be blocked at **Runswick Bay** by a very high tide.

The Cleveland Way is routed along the sandy beach, passing the blue-and-white **Runswick Bay Sailing Club** building at the far end.

Detour

In the event that the tide is fully in, the best course of action is to retire to a pub and wait an hour or two for the sea to recede, as detours inland are inconvenient.

Continue past a crumbling cliff at **Hob Holes** to find a river valley cutting through flaky beds of shale. Head inland through this valley, holding onto ropes and scrambling up crumbling slopes of shale for a short while. A steep flight of wooden steps leads up a bushy slope, out of the valley, and along the top of **High Cliff** around 100m (330ft).

Note that the line of a disused railway is a little further inland. The cliff path is pushed inland a little by a small gully choked with bushes. Turn left to follow a track through the hamlet of **Kettleness**. Apart from the first white building, keep seawards of all other buildings to pick up the cliff path as marked later.

KETTLENESS

The bare, rugged headland of Kettle Ness was once worked for alum, jet and ironstone. The previous village of Kettleness slumped into the sea in 1829. There was no loss of life, since the slump was gradual and the inhabitants were safely loaded onto a ship that was waiting for a consignment of alum. The alum works were destroyed along with the village, but the slump exposed more shale to be quarried, so a new works was built and operations began again within two years. There are no facilities in the village for walkers.

After following the grassy cliff-top path around the **Kettle Ness** headland, note that the **disused railway** is close to hand again. Watch it carefully to see it disappear into a tunnel. The tunnel – or tunnels, since there are

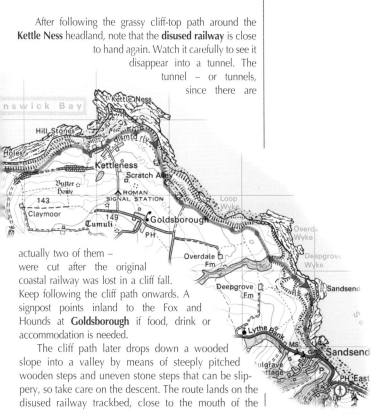

actually two of them – were cut after the original coastal railway was lost in a cliff fall. Keep following the cliff path onwards. A signpost points inland to the Fox and Hounds at **Goldsborough** if food, drink or accommodation is needed.

The cliff path later drops down a wooded slope into a valley by means of steeply pitched wooden steps and uneven stone steps that can be slippery, so take care on the descent. The route lands on the disused railway trackbed, close to the mouth of the

151

After leaving Runswick Bay, the Cleveland Way climbs towards Kettleness

Sandsend Tunnel, which is 1.5km (almost one mile) long. Turn left to walk along the old trackbed, through a cutting, along an embankment and passing old alum workings at **Sandsend Ness**, while looking ahead to Sandsend and Whitby. There are nature trail marker posts along the way. After a short wooded stretch, drop down steps on the left into a car park below the old station site and walk along a promenade path beside the A174 through **Sandsend**.

SANDSEND AND EAST ROW

These two little villages grew closer together when cottages were built for alum workers. The industry continued for over 250 years in Mulgrave Woods and around Sandsend Ness, ceasing operation in 1867. The coastal railway came past the villages in 1855, bored through headlands and straddling valleys on lofty viaducts, and bringing with it increased prosperity through tourist developments. Building projects virtually made the two villages into one. The railway line closed in 1958, but the sandy beach is close enough to Whitby for it to remain popular with local people and visitors.

Sandsend and neighbouring East Row offer hotel accommodation, a post office store, toilets, pub, restaurants, café and beach shop. There are regular Arriva bus X56 services to and from Whitby, as well as back along the coast to Runswick Bay, Staithes, Skelton, Guisborough and Middlesbrough.

DAY 7
Sandsend to Robin Hood's Bay

Start	Sandsend, grid ref 863125
Finish	Bay Hotel, Robin Hood's Bay, grid ref 953048
Distance	16km (10 miles)
Maps	OS Landranger 94, OS Explorer OL27
Terrain	After an initial road walk and urban walking, a reasonably easy cliff path leads onwards with only a few short, steep ascents and descents.
Refreshments	Plenty of pubs, cafés and restaurants around Whitby. Pub and café at Saltwick Bay. A few pubs, cafés and restaurants at Robin Hood's Bay.
Public Transport	Arriva bus X56 serves Whitby, Sandsend, Runswick Bay, Staithes, Skelton, Guisborough and Middlesbrough. Arriva bus 93 serves Whitby, Guisborough and Middlesbrough, as well as Robin Hood's Bay and Scarborough. Arriva trains run from Whitby to Kildale and Middlesbrough. Yorkshire Coastliner bus 840 links Whitby with Pickering, York and Leeds.

Plenty of people enjoy the easy stroll between Sandsend and Whitby, while the roller-coaster cliff path between Whitby and Robin Hood's Bay is also a popular choice for a day's walk. Few long-distance walkers would rush through Whitby without spending a while exploring the narrow streets and bustling harbourside. Although the din of amusement arcades and the constant mewling of gulls can be an assault on the ears, there is plenty of interest in this old whaling town. Even when the time comes to leave town, Whitby Abbey, perched high above the town, offers yet another distraction. Whatever happens, allow more time again in the evening for exploring Robin Hood's Bay, where a delightful heap of higgledy-piggledy houses clings to a steep slope and the last pub, the Bay Hotel, practically sits in the sea!

Cross the bridge between **Sandsend** and East Row and follow the main A174 gently uphill, drifting inland

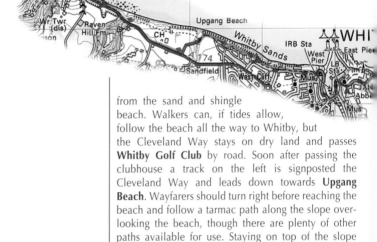

from the sand and shingle beach. Walkers can, if tides allow, follow the beach all the way to Whitby, but the Cleveland Way stays on dry land and passes **Whitby Golf Club** by road. Soon after passing the clubhouse a track on the left is signposted the Cleveland Way and leads down towards **Upgang Beach**. Wayfarers should turn right before reaching the beach and follow a tarmac path along the slope overlooking the beach, though there are plenty of other paths available for use. Staying on top of the slope leads past a series of hotels, including the Met. There is a prominent memorial to Captain Cook alongside a famous **Whalebone Arch**.

CAPTAIN COOK

After moving to Whitby from Staithes in 1747 James Cook was an apprentice seaman, lodging in an attic belonging to his Quaker master John Walker. Apprentices learned the art of navigation and seamanship through both lessons and hands-on experience on coal-carriers sailing to and from London. Cook's naval career commenced in 1755 and lasted almost 25 years until his untimely death in Hawaii in 1779. It is no doubt a testimony to Whitby's shipbuilding expertise that four of Captain Cook's ships were built in the town: *Endeavour*, *Resolution*, *Discovery* and *Adventure*. There is a replica of *Endeavour* in the harbour, where it can be boarded and inspected. It often sails out of the harbour for short trips. The Captain Cook Memorial Museum on Grape Lane charts the life and times of this remarkable explorer (there is an entrance charge).

Walk through the **Whalebone Arch** to find steps winding down a steep slope to the harbourside at **Whitby**. Head inland to cross the **Swing Bridge** spanning the tidal mouth of the River Esk. Alternatively, spend more time wandering around a veritable maze of narrow streets on both sides of the harbour to discover more about the heritage of the town. Bram Stoker would have been hard-pressed to find a better town to bring Dracula ashore!

After crossing the **Swing Bridge** turn left along a narrow, cobbled street lined with a variety of shops. Climb up the famous **199 Steps** to reach St Mary's Church – **Caedmon's Cross** stands at the top of the steps, just to the left. Either explore the churchyard and church, founded in the 12th century, or continue straight ahead towards **Whitby Abbey**. Next, either turn right to visit the abbey or keep straight on alongside the tall wall surrounding it. Turn left along a path beside some buildings to return to the cliff-top Cleveland Way.

Follow the cliff path onwards to **Saltwick Bay** and enjoy the open coastal scenery again. **Saltwick Nab** is a prominent humpbacked headland, but one that is largely the result of the quarrying of alum shales. There is access to the beach if required, otherwise walk along the road through the **Whitby Holiday Village** where there is a campsite, shop, pub and café. Just as the road leaves the site a Cleveland Way signpost points left along the grassy cliff path. There is a view down on the isolated sea stack

Map continues p.158

155

WHITBY WHALERS

Whitby developed greatly as a town from the mid-18th to mid-19th centuries as its fishing fleets turned to whaling. Whalers spent months at sea and did not always return with a catch. Whale blubber was highly prized, the oil rendered from it giving a bright and fairly soot-free light when burned. Women of the era would have more than enough reason to curse their whalebone corsets, but the trade allowed the town to prosper immensely. The whalebone arch was presented to the town by Norway, suggesting that the Whitby whalers always disposed of every last part of their catch!

WHITBY

Facilities in Whitby include all types of accommodation, including a youth hostel and nearby campsite. There are banks with ATMs, a post office, toilets, and an abundance of pubs, restaurants, cafés and takeaways. The tourist information centre is near Endeavour Wharf, tel 01947 602674. There are plenty of bus services, but perhaps the most useful are the Arriva bus X56 back to Sandsend, Runswick Bay, Staithes, Skelton, Guisborough and Middlesbrough, and bus 93 back to Guisborough and Middlesbrough and ahead to Robin Hood's Bay and Scarborough. Yorkshire Coastliner bus 840 runs across the moors to Pickering, York and Leeds and Arriva trains run inland to Kildale and Middlesbrough.

WHITBY ABBEY

St Hilda founded Whitby Abbey in the year 657. According to legend, fossilised ammonites were snakes that were turned to stone by St Hilda! The Danes destroyed the abbey in 867, another foundation of 1078 was also unsuccessful, and much of what is seen today dates from the 12th century. However, the original abbey was founded in time to host the Synod of Whitby in the year 664. At this synod the Celtic and Roman Christian traditions, separated during the Dark Ages, settled some of the differences that each had accrued over the years, and agreed a method for calculating the movable feast of Easter. The abbey is also famous for one of its early lay brothers, Caedmon, who was inspired to sing in a dream one night, and whose words are the earliest English Christian verse to be written down. (There is an entrance charge.)

A cobbled road leads to the famous '199 steps' leading up and out of Whitby

of **Black Nab**, also the result of alum-shale quarrying. The twisted wreckage of the *Admiral Von Tromp*, which ran aground in 1976, can be seen near the beach.

Keep to the seaward side of a **foghorn**, but follow a path on the landward side of a **lighthouse**. Climb higher along the cliff path to around 90m (295ft) above sea level. The path basically rolls along, rising and falling fairly gently, with rugged cliffs down to the left and fields rising to the right. There are, however, a couple of steep-sided wooded valleys to cross around **Maw Wyke Hole**. Also, at a point where a path heads inland to Hawsker, there is a bench and a small garden, but no habitation in view. (The Coast to Coast Walk, last seen on the highest part of the North York Moors, now joins the Cleveland Way.) The path climbs a bit then swings round and down through a gentle valley at **Bay Ness**. Enjoy views back along the cliff coast.

Walk around **Ness Point** to see Robin Hood's Bay, but only after passing below the old coastguard hut and entering the **Rocket Post Field**. The path runs to the top end of the village where a left turn at the Grosvenor Hotel leads down the B1447. Walk down a steep and narrow road, winding through the jumbled houses and cottages of **Robin Hood's Bay**, to reach the rocky shore at a stout sea wall that holds the village in place. The Bay Hotel bears a plaque marking the end of the Coast to Coast Walk, but the Cleveland Way is still good for a couple more days of splendid walking.

The Bay Hotel rises straight from the rocky, fossil-rich shore, and has had one ship wrecked against its wall and another poke its bowsprit straight through a window. One thing seems fairly certain – Robin Hood never had any association with the village.

ROBIN HOOD'S BAY

This charming and curiously complex village has a history of smuggling during which the villagers often engaged in hostilities with the revenue men. Local folk claim that a bolt of silk could be passed through secret cupboards and doorways from the shore to the top of the village without once seeing the light of day. They also tell of an incident when smugglers and revenue men waged a pitched battle in the bay and it was possible to read newsprint at night from the flash of gunpowder.

Facilities include plenty of accommodation, including a nearby youth hostel and campsite, a post office, toilets, pubs, restaurants, cafés and a few shops. Arriva bus 93 runs from the top end of the village ahead to Scarborough, and back towards Whitby, Guisborough and Middlesbrough.

Robin Hood's Bay is a delightful old village with a tradition of smuggling

DAY 8
Robin Hood's Bay to Scarborough

Start	Bay Hotel, Robin Hood's Bay, grid ref 953048
Finish	Corner Café, Scarborough, grid ref 037897
Distance	23.5km (14.5 miles)
Maps	OS Landrangers 94 and 101, OS Explorer OL27
Terrain	Gentle cliff walking and field paths to Ravenscar, then the cliff path features several short ascents and descents, with some short, steep slopes.
Refreshments	Pub and café at Ravenscar, pub near Hayburn Wyke and another at Scalby Mills. Every type of pub, restaurant, café and takeaway is available around Scarborough.
Public Transport	Arriva bus 93 runs between Robin Hood's Bay and Scarborough, as well as back to Whitby, Guisborough and Middlesbrough. Scarborough & District bus 16 operates daily except Sunday between Ravenscar and Scarborough. Bus 3A runs daily except Sunday from the Sea Life Centre at Scalby Mills to Scarborough. There is also a miniature railway from the Sea Life Centre to Peasholm Park in Scarborough. In the summer frequent open-top buses run around the Scarborough seafront. Yorkshire Coastliner bus 843 runs from Scarborough to York and Leeds. Railway services offer connections throughout the country.

As Robin Hood's Bay recedes from view, the cliff-top village of Ravenscar looms ahead. An entire resort town was once planned on top of Old Peak, and although hardly any of it was built some of the roads that were laid out are still clearly visible. The sloping cliffs covered with thick woodland scrub make an ideal wildlife habitat, particularly around Beast Cliff. There is an attractive boulder beach with a small waterfall at Hayburn Wyke. Beyond Cloughton Wyke the Cleveland Way leaves the North York Moors National Park, but the cliff coastline is attractive all the way to Scalby Mills. Ahead lies the busy seaside resort of Scarborough. There is no waymarked route for the Cleveland Way through town, but a couple of options can be considered for the next day.

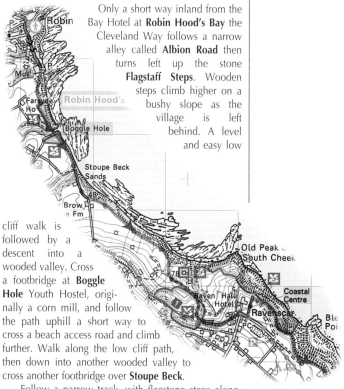

Only a short way inland from the Bay Hotel at **Robin Hood's Bay** the Cleveland Way follows a narrow alley called **Albion Road** then turns left up the stone **Flagstaff Steps**. Wooden steps climb higher on a bushy slope as the village is left behind. A level and easy low cliff walk is followed by a descent into a wooded valley. Cross a footbridge at **Boggle Hole** Youth Hostel, originally a corn mill, and follow the path uphill a short way to cross a beach access road and climb further. Walk along the low cliff path, then down into another wooded valley to cross another footbridge over **Stoupe Beck**.

Follow a narrow track, with flagstone steps alongside, up a wooded slope. Pass **Stoupe Bank Farm** and follow its access road until a slight dip has been crossed. Turn left as signposted Cleveland Way to pick up the cliff path again. Views back along the coast reveal that the village of Robin Hood's Bay is dwindling, while ahead the village of Ravenscar draws nearer. The path is broad and grassy, running around 60m (200ft) above sea level. It suddenly heads uphill inland, through fields, then left along a **farm track**. Fork right up a **concrete track** at a junction, then fork right again up a **clear path** flanked by broom and gorse bushes. The path rises through woods

Map continues p.163

161

and continues along a track studded with bricks that were made locally and stamped with the name **Ravenscar**. Walk to the entrance gate of the Raven Hall Hotel and turn right along **Station Road**, around 190m (625ft). Turn left as signposted along a wide and stony track to regain the cliff path.

RAVENSCAR

The Romans built a signal station at Ravenscar more or less where the Raven Hall Hotel now stands. Alum mining was a profitable occupation in the area, leaving the cliffs around Old Peak looking rather bare. In the 1890s there was a grand scheme to create a new tourist resort here, but despite a road system and drains being laid very few investors bought plots or built properties and the scheme ground to a halt in the 1920s. Facilities, however, include a hotel, bed-and-breakfast and campsite, as well as a post office, toilets, pub, seasonal tearoom and a National Trust information centre. Scarborough & District bus 16 links Ravenscar with Scarborough daily except Sunday.

Chunky cobbles are piled high on the beach around lovely Hayburn Wyke

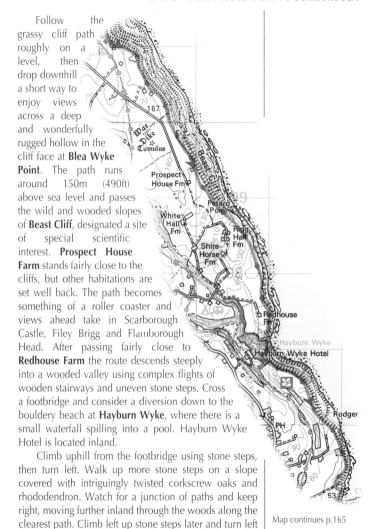

Follow the grassy cliff path roughly on a level, then drop downhill a short way to enjoy views across a deep and wonderfully rugged hollow in the cliff face at **Blea Wyke Point**. The path runs around 150m (490ft) above sea level and passes the wild and wooded slopes of **Beast Cliff**, designated a site of special scientific interest. **Prospect House Farm** stands fairly close to the cliffs, but other habitations are set well back. The path becomes something of a roller coaster and views ahead take in Scarborough Castle, Filey Brigg and Flamborough Head. After passing fairly close to **Redhouse Farm** the route descends steeply into a wooded valley using complex flights of wooden stairways and uneven stone steps. Cross a footbridge and consider a diversion down to the bouldery beach at **Hayburn Wyke**, where there is a small waterfall spilling into a pool. Hayburn Wyke Hotel is located inland.

Climb uphill from the footbridge using stone steps, then turn left. Walk up more stone steps on a slope covered with intriguingly twisted corkscrew oaks and rhododendron. Watch for a junction of paths and keep right, moving further inland through the woods along the clearest path. Climb left up stone steps later and turn left at the top. Climb further uphill to leave the woods and continue along the top of the wooded slope, looking

Map continues p.165

163

A slender waterfall spills into a
rock pool on the beach at Hayburn Wyke

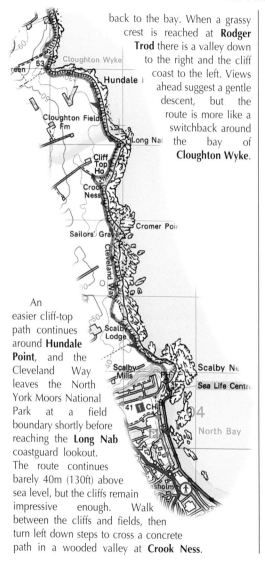

back to the bay. When a grassy crest is reached at **Rodger Trod** there is a valley down to the right and the cliff coast to the left. Views ahead suggest a gentle descent, but the route is more like a switchback around the bay of **Cloughton Wyke**.

An easier cliff-top path continues around **Hundale Point**, and the Cleveland Way leaves the North York Moors National Park at a field boundary shortly before reaching the **Long Nab** coastguard lookout. The route continues barely 40m (130ft) above sea level, but the cliffs remain impressive enough. Walk between the cliffs and fields, then turn left down steps to cross a concrete path in a wooded valley at **Crook Ness**.

A view around North Bay from the flowery Queens Parade in Scarborough

Climb up steps and continue along the cliff path. There are quite a few little ups and downs and the route passes the Sailor's Grave on **Cromer Point**. A signpost reading Footpath to Burniston Road and pointing inland marks the start of the Tabular Hills Walk that would lead walkers 81km (50 miles) back to Helmsley. The Cleveland Way, however, continues to hug the cliff coast to **Scalby Nab**. Either walk around this final promontory or cut behind it and follow a path straight down a bushy slope to reach a footbridge. The **Old Scalby Mills** pub is immediately to hand.

There are buses into Scarborough from here and the **Sea Life Centre** is an immediate distraction. There is even a miniature railway tempting walkers to take a ride, but it is simple enough to walk along **North Bay Promenade** to approach the town. The promenade is traffic-free and leads to the **Corner Café** on the outskirts of **Scarborough**, not far from popular Peasholm Park. There are no markers or signposts for the Cleveland Way so walkers are free to head in any direction, and the ultimate choice of route will largely depend on where you are staying overnight in town.

SCARBOROUGH

The emergence of Scarborough as a premier holiday resort can be traced to the promotion of its spa waters. In 1626 a local doctor extolled the benefits of drinking the water, making so many claims about its curative properties that one must suspect quackery! However, visitors flocked to the town and before long the benefits of sea air and sea bathing were also being promoted. So enthusiastic were the crowds of holidaymakers that more and more facilities had to be built to cater for them. The arrival of the railway in 1845 boosted the tourism trade and the town remains a busy and bustling place to this day.

Facilities around Scarborough include a wide range of accommodation options, from splendid hotels to humble bed-and-breakfasts, as well as a youth hostel at Scalby Mills and nearby campsites. There are banks with ATMs, post offices, toilets, and an abundance of pubs, restaurants, cafés and takeaways to suit all tastes (though in most cases it's 'chips with everything'). As a shopping centre Scarborough has the greatest choice of any place visited along the Cleveland Way. There is a tourist information centre opposite the railway station, tel 01723 373333, and trains run to a number of destinations in the country. Yorkshire Coastliner bus 843 links Scarborough with York and Leeds. Arriva bus 93 operates back to Robin Hood's Bay, Whitby, Guisborough and Middlesbrough. Scarborough & District bus 16 runs between Scarborough and Ravenscar. East Yorkshire buses 120 and 121 run from Scarborough to Filey, and there are plenty of other buses operating all around town, including open-top summer buses from North Bay to South Bay.

DAY 9
Scarborough to Filey

Start	Corner Café, Scarborough, grid ref 037897
Finish	Coble Landing, Filey, grid ref 120809
Distance	18km (11 miles)
Maps	OS Landranger 101, OS Explorer 301
Terrain	Urban walking gives way to a rugged, wooded slope followed by fairly straightforward cliff walking.
Refreshments	Plenty of refreshment options around Scarborough. Beach hut and surf shop at Cayton Bay. Plenty of pubs, restaurants and cafés around Filey.
Public Transport	Scarborough & District bus services run all around Scarborough, while East Yorkshire buses 120 and 121 operate between Scarborough and Filey. Arriva trains run between Scarborough and Filey.

The Cleveland Way is not waymarked or signposted through Scarborough. Indeed, some writers have suggested getting a bus through town rather than walking, but this seems remiss given that Scarborough has plenty of interest that is best discovered on foot. Walkers might opt to head straight through the town centre, or follow Marine Drive around the headland, but for those who would like to appreciate some of Scarborough's history and heritage a route is offered below that takes in a few of its more prominent features. Once clear of the town, wooded slopes and fairly easy cliff walking leads onwards to Filey Brigg. For some obscure reason the Cleveland Way ends in the middle of nowhere, before reaching the impressive headland of Filey Brigg, and walkers find themselves embarking on the course of the Yorkshire Wolds Way in order to reach the end of the day's walk at Filey.

There is no waymarked route for the Cleveland Way through **Scarborough**. Walkers could follow **Royal Albert Drive** alongside North Bay, then **Marine Drive** around the

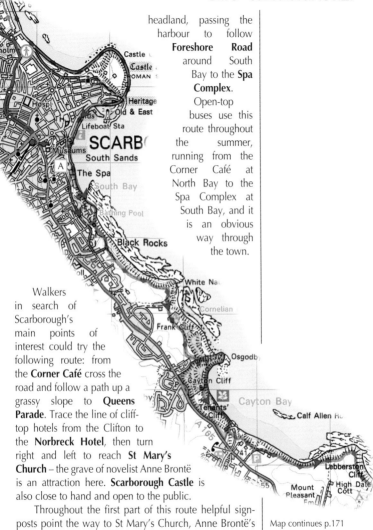

headland, passing the harbour to follow **Foreshore Road** around South Bay to the **Spa Complex**.

Open-top buses use this route throughout the summer, running from the Corner Café at North Bay to the Spa Complex at South Bay, and it is an obvious way through the town.

Walkers in search of Scarborough's main points of interest could try the following route: from the **Corner Café** cross the road and follow a path up a grassy slope to **Queens Parade**. Trace the line of cliff-top hotels from the Clifton to the **Norbreck Hotel**, then turn right and left to reach **St Mary's Church** – the grave of novelist Anne Brontë is an attraction here. **Scarborough Castle** is also close to hand and open to the public.

Throughout the first part of this route helpful sign-posts point the way to St Mary's Church, Anne Brontë's Grave and Scarborough Castle. Next, follow signposts for the Old Town, Sands and Harbour, walking down

Map continues p.171

SCARBOROUGH CASTLE

Bronze Age settlers are though to have been the first people to fortify the headland at Scarborough. The Romans operated a signal station on a line of sight linked with other coastal signal stations at Ravenscar and Filey Brigg. In the 12th century Scarborough Castle was built on the headland. The castle withstood a 20-day siege during the Pilgrimage of Grace in 1536, but surrendered after a year-long siege during the Civil War in 1645. The ruins of the castle can be visited while exploring the town (there is an entrance charge).

Castlegate to reach the **Old Harbour**. Continue along **Foreshore Road** around South Bay, passing what is by far the busiest beach in town. (Scarborough's main shopping area can be reached by climbing inland, perhaps walking up Blands Cliff or using one of the cliff lifts for easy access.) Continue to the **Spa Complex** at the end of **South Bay** and consider options for leaving town.

There is a low-level promenade path leaving the **Spa Complex**, and anyone following this will find that a clear gravel track later rises uphill to a car park on **Sea Cliff Road**, but bear in mind that heavy seas can overwhelm this path and care must be exercised. Alternatively, a safer network of paths crisscrosses wooded and shrubby areas on **South Cliff** where signposts point uphill to the **Esplanade**, which can in turn be followed to **Holbeck Hill**. Turn left and left again to reach a car park at the end of **Sea Cliff Road.**

THE HOLBECK LANDSLIDE

The Holbeck Hall Hotel was built as a private residence in 1880, and later converted into a hotel. Unfortunately the ground beneath the building was essentially unstable and began to slump on 3 June 1993, an event that was documented by TV crews as it happened. The following day the hotel was in ruins and about a million tonnes of material had slumped into the sea in a huge bulge. An information board beside the Sea Cliff Road car park shows before and after pictures of the event, and the area has since been landscaped.

The Cleveland Way is signposted for Filey below the car park, where a narrow path leads onto a wooded slope – be sure

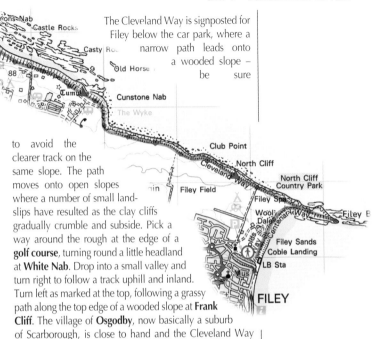

to avoid the clearer track on the same slope. The path moves onto open slopes where a number of small land-slips have resulted as the clay cliffs gradually crumble and subside. Pick a way around the rough at the edge of a **golf course**, turning round a little headland at **White Nab**. Drop into a small valley and turn right to follow a track uphill and inland. Turn left as marked at the top, following a grassy path along the top edge of a wooded slope at **Frank Cliff**. The village of **Osgodby**, now basically a suburb of Scarborough, is close to hand and the Cleveland Way passes close to a house near the edge of the cliff.

Follow a path down into the woods near **Knipe Point**. Keep strictly to the marked path as there are other paths leading down to the beach at **Cayton Bay**. (Geologists might like to detour from here down to Cornelian Bay to pick semi-precious cornelian from the beach.) The wood-lands obscure views at first, but there are fine outlooks over the bay and cliffs later. Note the Second World War pill-boxes at intervals, some of which have tilted or toppled as the clay cliffs on which they were built have subsided. The path appears to head for a beach, but actually turns right and climbs up a steep, stone-pitched path on **Tenants Cliff** to run at a higher level. Drop down to a beach access road and cross it, climbing up the other side to pass a caravan site. There is a beach hut down the road and bus stops up the road near a junction with the busy A165.

Walk past a cliff-top cottage and follow a grassy path parallel to an access track serving a row of houses. A **surf shop** a short way inland sells sweets, ice cream and drinks. The path gradually climbs over **Lebberston Cliff**, some 80m (260ft) above sea level. There are fine views along the cliff coast back towards Scarborough on the descent. Turn round a headland and follow the path gently uphill along **Gristhorpe Cliff**, passing a caravan site. Turn around **Cunstone Nab** and continue along **Newbiggin Cliff** to enjoy an easy, open grassy cliff path. By the time **Filey Brigg** is reached there is a monumental stone marker commemorating both the Cleveland Way and the Yorkshire Wolds Way. Walk out onto the grassy crest of Filey Brigg and enjoy views of the rocky tidal reef projecting into the sea.

FILEY BRIGG

The grassy top of Filey Brigg has been crumbling steadily over the centuries and will one day be gone, leaving only the hard calcareous gritstone bedrock beneath. A Roman signal station and 12th-century castle have already been lost as the clay cliffs gradually crumble, and walkers are now forbidden to continue along the badly worn clay ridge leading down to the rocky slabs of Brigg End. If you want to go to the very end of the Brigg you should do it by walking along Filey Sands when the tide is out, but bear in mind that the rocks are covered in slippery seaweed and big waves break across them without warning. There is an emergency telephone for those who find themselves marooned out on the point or spot anyone in obvious difficulty or danger.

The seaside resort of Filey is clearly in view and there is an easy, grassy cliff-top path leading through the **Filey Country Park** in that direction. A flight of steps leads down into **Wool Dale**, where there is beach access if required, and up the other side. The cliff path passes above Filey Sailing Club then a zigzag path leads down a wooded slope to a road junction at the **Coble Landing**. Walkers who wish to end their exploration of the Cleveland Way here can head into **Filey** in search of

food, drink and accommodation. Those who wish to continue along the course of the Yorkshire Wolds Way will find the route signposted up steps behind the toilets across the road.

A view of the crumbling headland of Filey Brigg from the Filey Country Park

FILEY

Filey is another little fishing town that has turned its attention to tourism. On the Coble Landing fishing boats lie on trailers beside amusement arcades, as if the transition is not yet complete. The town is fairly small, yet supports a good range of services, whether walkers are at the end of the Cleveland Way, the start of the Yorkshire Wolds Way, or just passing through.

Facilities include a good range of accommodation and a nearby campsite. There are banks with ATMs, a post office, toilets, plenty of pubs, restaurants, cafés and takeaways, as well as shops. The museum should be visited by anyone wanting a potted history of the town and there is a tourist information centre on John Street, tel 01723 518000. Arriva trains run back to Scarborough as well as to Hull, while East Yorkshire buses 120 and 121 also run between Filey and Scarborough. Yorkshire Coastliner bus 845 links Filey with York and Leeds.

*Lebberston cliff and its curious pillar outcrop
are seen on the way to Filey*

THE WALKING PARSON

The Rev Arthur Cooper was born in 1827 and took up walking as a means of getting around his parish while he was a curate in Durham. At the age of 60, shortly after taking an appointment in the parish of Filey, he decided to walk from Filey to Rome. He practiced by walking from Filey to London in less than a week, taking the Sunday service before leaving Filey and returning to take the following Sunday service. This was simply to prove to himself that he was capable of covering long distances. He then walked from Filey to Rome in only seven weeks, declaring, 'Good-bye all ye vampires of modern travel. Good-bye insolent cab men and tip-loving porters. Good-bye misdirected luggage and dusty railway carriages.' Several more European treks followed, mostly along car-free roads, and Cooper also wrote books and gave talks about his journeys. Although teetotal he was in the habit of stomping into pubs and ordering glasses of whisky, which he poured into his shoes while still wearing them, declaring, 'It makes the foot and sock and shoe all pliable together.' By the time of his death in 1920, at the grand old age of 93, opinions were divided as to whether he was a complete eccentric or the greatest British walker of his time, or both. He can make the rest of us feel, even after walking 400km (250 miles), like mere novices!

Coble Landing at Filey, where boats are brought up alongside amusement arcades

APPENDIX 1: Route Summary

The Yorkshire Wolds Way National Trail

Walk	km	miles	cumulative km	cumulative miles
Hessle to Welton	10.5	6.5	10.5	6.5
Welton to South Cave	11	7	21.5	13.5
South Cave to North Newbald	9	5.5	30.5	19
North Newbald to Arras	5	3	35.5	22
Arras to Market Weighton	4.5	3	40	25
Market Weighton to Millington	14.5	9	54.5	34
Millington to Huggate	13	8	67.5	42
Huggate to Fridaythorpe	4	2.5	71.5	44.5
Fridaythorpe to Thixendale	6.5	4	78	48.5
Thixendale to Wharram le Street	8	5	86.5	53.5
Wharram to Wintringham	10.5	6.5	97	60
Wintringham to Sherburn	10.5	6.5	107.5	66.5
Sherburn to Muston	18.5	11.5	126	78
Muston to Filey	4	2.5	130	80.5
Filey to Scalby Mills (Cleveland Way)	19	12	149	92.5

The Tabular Hills Walk

Walk	km	miles	cumulative km	cumulative miles
Scalby Mills to Givendale Head	18	11	18	11
Givendale Head to Levisham	16	10	34	21
Levisham to Cropton	16	10	50	31
Cropton to Hutton-le-Hole	9	5.5	59	36.5
Hutton-le-Hole to Fadmoor	4	2.5	63	39
Fadmoor to Helmsley	18	11	81	50

The Cleveland Way National Trail

Walk	km	miles	cumulative km	cumulative miles
Helmsley to Sutton Bank	17	10.5	17	10.5
Sutton Bank to Osmotherley	18.5	11.5	35.5	22
Osmotherley to Carlton Bank	11	7	46.5	29
Carlton Bank to Clay Bank	7	4	53.5	33
Clay Bank to Kildale	15	9.5	68.5	42.5
Kildale to Slapewath	16	10	84.5	52.5
Slapewath to Saltburn	8	5	92.5	57.5
Saltburn to Staithes	14	9	106.5	66.5
Staithes to Runswick Bay	5.5	3.5	112	70
Runswick Bay to Sandsend	7.5	4.5	119.5	74.5
Sandsend to Whitby	5	3	124.5	77.5
Whitby to Robin Hood's Bay	11	7	135.5	84.5
Robin Hood's Bay to Ravenscar	6	3.5	141.5	88
Ravenscar to Scarborough	17.5	11	159	99
Scarborough to Filey	18	11	177	110
Cumulative totals for all three trails			**407km**	**252.5 miles**

178

Saltwick Nab's shape was determined during many years alum mining (Cleveland Way, Day 7)

APPENDIX 2:
Useful Information

TOURIST INFORMATION CENTRES

The Yorkshire Wolds Way National Trail

Hull	Paragon Street, Hull, ☎ 01482 223559
Humber Bridge	North Bank Viewing Area, ☎ 01482 640852
Malton	Market Place, Malton, ☎ 01653 600048
Filey	Evron Centre, John Street, Filey, ☎ 01723 518000

The Tabular Hills Walk

Scarborough	Valley Bridge Road, Scarborough, ☎ 01723 73333
Hutton-le-Hole	Ryedale Folk Museum, ☎ 01751 17367
Helmsley	Market Place, Helmsley, ☎ 01439 70173

The Cleveland Way National Trail

Sutton Bank	National Park Centre, ☎ 01845 597426
Great Ayton	High Green Car Park, ☎ 01642 722835
Guisborough	Church Street, Guisborough, ☎ 01287 633801
Saltburn-by-the-Sea	Station Buildings, Saltburn, ☎ 01287-622422
Whitby	Langbourne Road, Whitby, ☎ 01947-602674
Robin Hood's Bay	Old Coastguard Station, ☎ 01947-885900
Ravenscar	National Trust Centre, ☎ 01723-870138
Scarborough	Valley Bridge Road, Scarborough, ☎ 01723-373333
Filey	Evron Centre, John Street, Filey, ☎ 01723-518000

WEBSITES

The Cleveland Way National Trail **www.nationaltrail.co.uk/clevelandway**
The Yorkshire Wolds Way National Trail
www.nationaltrail.co.uk/yorkshirewoldsway
A good website covering the North York Moors National Park is
www.visitthemoors.co.uk.
Online timetables for both major bus companies serving the area – East Yorkshire
Motor Services (which operates Scarborough & District buses) and Arriva buses –
can be checked at **www.arriva.co.uk** or **www.eyms.co.uk**.
Rail services throughout Britain can be checked at **www.nationalrail.co.uk**.

NATIONAL TRAIL INFORMATION

The Yorkshire Wolds Way Accommodation and Information Guide
The Cleveland Way Accommodation and Information Guide
Both available from tourist information centres, or by post from:
The North York Moors National Park Authority
The Old Vicarage
Helmsley
York YO62 5BP
Telephone 01439 770657

TELEPHONE NUMBERS

National Rail Enquiries, ☎ 0845 7484950. Timetable information for rail services throughout Britain.
Traveline, ☎ 0870 6082608. Provides information about public transport links throughout the country.
National Taxi Hotline, ☎ 0800 654321. Free service linking the caller with the nearest taxi operator in the scheme, allowing you to check their rates before confirming a booking.

The Sea Cut leads far inland from Scalby Mills to Mowthorpe Bridge (Day 1 of the Tabular Hills Walk)

NOTES

NOTES

NOTES

NOTES

NOTES

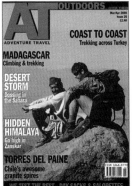

LISTING OF CICERONE GUIDES

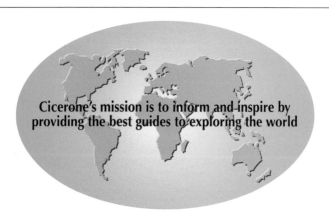

Cicerone's mission is to inform and inspire by
providing the best guides to exploring the world

Since its foundation over 30 years ago, Cicerone has specialised in publishing guidebooks and has built a reputation for quality and reliability. It now publishes nearly 300 guides to the major destinations for outdoor enthusiasts, including Europe, UK and the rest of the world.

Written by leading and committed specialists, Cicerone guides are recognised as the most authoritative. They are full of information, maps and illustrations so that the user can plan and complete a successful and safe trip or expedition – be it a long face climb, a walk over Lakeland fells, an alpine traverse, a Himalayan trek or a ramble in the countryside.

With a thorough introduction to assist planning, clear diagrams, maps and colour photographs to illustrate the terrain and route, and accurate and detailed text, Cicerone guides are designed for ease of use and access to the information.

If the facts on the ground change, or there is any aspect of a guide that you think we can improve, we are always delighted to hear from you.

Cicerone Press
2 Police Square Milnthorpe Cumbria LA7 7PY
Tel:01539 562 069   Fax:01539 563 417
e-mail:info@cicerone.co.uk   web:www.cicerone.co.uk

CICERONE